The Debt
and the Deficit

Robert Heilbroner
and Peter Bernstein

The Debt
and the Deficit

False Alarms / Real Possibilities

W · W · NORTON & COMPANY

NEW YORK · LONDON

Pages 108–9: From Herbert Stein, *The AEI Economist*,
December 1988, pp. 1–7. Permission granted from the
American Enterprise Institute for Public Policy Research.

First Edition

ISBN 0-393-02752-X

0-393-30611-9 {PBK.}

W. W. Norton & Company, Inc., 500 Fifth Avenue, New York, N. Y. 10110
W. W. Norton & Company Ltd., 37 Great Russell Street, London WC1B 3NU

1 2 3 4 5 6 7 8 9 0

For Kate, Peter, Zeke, Jonah, and Bobby

Contents

9

Contents

I

A Personal Preface

A LITTLE MORE than twenty-five years ago
President John F. Kennedy proposed a $10
billion deficit to stimulate a sagging economy. The proposal was met with cries of horror and consternation. A
popular evangelist was moved to declare deficit spending
as "the greatest moral danger facing our country at the
moment." The chairman of the House Appropriations
Committee warned that deficits led inexorably to the de-
bauchment of the currency. The *New York Times* senior
Washington correspondent spoke ominously of a grim
reckoning ahead.

Fired up with the reformist zeal of the times, we sat
down to write a "primer" on deficit spending whose purpose was to introduce the evangelist, the chairman, and
the *New York Times* to economics. A draft was sent to
Walter W. Heller, then chairman of the Council of Economic Advisors, and, perhaps at his suggestion, President
Kennedy himself read the manuscript. (He even found an
oversight in it.) We had momentary visions of the president explaining his proposals to the American public

while holding aloft *A Primer on Government Spending,* but terrible events intervened.

In the wake of the Kennedy assassination, Congress passed the Kennedy tax cut, but already the economy had begun to recover spontaneously. The government ran only a tiny deficit in 1964, the year of the tax cut, and none thereafter until 1967. Thus the dire predictions were never tested. The moral fiber of the nation decayed for other reasons; the U.S. currency lost its value slowly as it had been doing for some time; and several grim reckonings were faced—but not on the matter of the deficit. The *Primer,* incidentally, sold very well.

There are some obvious similarities between those days and these. Americans are as transfixed by the deficit today as they were a quarter of a century ago. We hear the same moral outrage, the same warnings about debauchery, the same grimness as to "reckonings." But things are also very different. Today's deficit is much, much bigger than Kennedy's $10 billion (worth about $40 billion in today's dollars). Our deficit is not being deliberately put forward to stimulate the economy, but is imposed on us in ways we do not understand. Most economists on record in the 1960s supported the deficit as a constructive move; most economists on record today are convinced that the deficit is a problem that must be gotten rid of at all costs.* Finally, we face national problems that were unimaginable in Kennedy's day: how to find a place in the world economy; how to live with an economy that seems to be simul-

---

*Among the eminent exceptions is Robert Eisner, president of the American Economic Association for 1988. We gratefully acknowledge his intellectual leadership.

taneously inflation-prone and sluggish; how to cope with orgies of self-indulgence side by side with barrens of misery.

For all these differences, our purpose today is much as it was a quarter of a century ago: to instill a little understanding in place of fears—worse, frights. Frights are states of mind that can prevent us from meeting real challenges with realistic responses. Not one person in a thousand can tell you why either the debt or the deficit is a threat to this country, but four hundred and forty out of a thousand will tell you that both are America's most immediate danger. Here are the results of a Los Angeles Times Mirror poll of 2,022 voters across the nation who were asked in late 1988 to identify the *one* issue that should be the Bush administration's top priority:

Reduce the deficit	44%
Protect Americans jobs from foreign competition	20%
Strengthen programs that help families	15%
Negotiate further arms reductions with the USSR	12%
Improve protection of the environment	8%

That poll represents the sentiment that has moved us to write this book. The deficit is a very real problem, but by no sober reasoning can "reducing it" be the top priority for this country. It is certainly possible to amass a debt that will cripple this country or to run up deficits that would plunge us into economic chaos, but there is nothing in the immediate situation to warrant such imaginings. That is why "false alarms" appears in the subtitle of our book.

The only remedy for such a frightened state of mind is

explanations that are simple but accurate, facts that will defuse unreasoning panic, and arguments that will stand up under the most skeptical examination. That is what we have tried to provide in these pages.

We are writing for two audiences. The first and by far the more important are interested Americans who are concerned about public issues, but even more concerned because the number-one public issue is beyond their grasp. For them we have written a kind of primer—a book that will not be hard to take, even though parts of it toward the end may not be altogether easy. At any rate, this part of our audience will discover that our book presumes absolutely no familiarity with financial and economic terms, even the ones we all use every day. It takes for granted only the general intelligence and genuine interest of its readers.

The second audience is made up of our fellow professionals, for whom much of this book will be very "easy"— but perhaps hard to take. We ask only that they set aside the assurance that comes of knowing that the great preponderance (but not all) of expert opinion is on their side, and that they read our short exposition for its internal consistency and logic and for its accord with facts.

For both audiences, it may be helpful to know in advance the direction in which our discussion will proceed. We begin with a short chapter describing how the United States stumbled into the deficit crisis, for never was there a national state of affairs that arrived so unexpectedly and whose causes are still so widely misperceived.

Then we take a few chapters to define some basic

terms—mainly "debt" and "deficit"—and to set forth some basic concepts. These may come as more of a surprise to general readers than to economists, but no harm will be done by a review of fundamental facts and relationships. Indeed, such respected economists as Milton Friedman and Herbert Stein, and so distinguished a financier as Walter Wriston, have been moved to write letters or articles protesting the general misperception of basic facts.[1] We will quote them when we need their support.

We then take up two fundamental questions having to do with the dangers of the deficit: "crowding out" and "living beyond our means"—the linked issues of our savings shortfall and our import surplus. We conclude with a plea to reduce the deficit from the status of a fright to that of an economic concern, to turn off the alarm bells, and to consider whether we should not change our national accounting system to make the prudent management of our economy understandable by the people for whom it is being managed.

Finally, a point that may have occurred to many readers: Is it not curious that no clear-cut signs of harm have come from having failed to do anything about the deficit, despite five years of hand-wringing? Perhaps, to listen to those who do worry about the deficit, that is precisely what is so insidious about it, eating away at our economy like a swarm of termites invisibly consuming a house. But the absence of any dramatic comeuppance also suggests that this most "pressing" of America's problems will wait a while before it brings the economy crashing down about our ears. Certainly the problem will last long enough for people to read this short book and think about its contents—after which, if our arguments ring true, we can turn to dealing with the deficit and the debt with the immeasurable relief that comes from understanding what we are talking about.

2

How We Got into This Mess

WHEN Ronald Reagan became president of the United States in January 1981 no one had any idea that things would turn out as they did.

Not one businessman, banker, political leader, or economist anticipated that during the next eight years the United States would spend $1.3 trillion more than it received in tax revenues, giving us a total national debt of $2.6 trillion. No banker, businessman, economist, or political leader foresaw that because of that horrendous debt we would run up another debt of almost a trillion dollars—the result of buying some $800 billion worth of more goods and services from other nations than we sold in return. Nor did a single businessman, political leader, economist, or banker expect the American economy—that marvelous productivity machine—to become a world-class invalid in less than a decade, once again because of that damnable debt.

Are these concerns to be believed? They are not. But neither are they to be dismissed out of hand. Clearly something is wrong with a nation whose finances are out of control; and there is certainly something wrong with a situation that worries so many people so deeply, for good reasons or bad.

We must find out how we got ourselves into such a mess. How could we have acted so recklessly and with so little regard for the future? What happened in a mere eight years to confront us with such a direful and utterly unforeseen state of affairs?

Our story begins in late 1979, in an economy suffering from the symptoms of an increasingly worrisome inflationary ailment. The ailment, to be sure, was a good deal older. In the late 1960s, Lyndon B. Johnson stepped up expenditures to prosecute the unpopular Vietnam War, but he refrained from raising taxes. As a consequence, inflation began to appear as part of the normal workings of the economy. In 1971, Richard Nixon, the first president to become exercised about inflation, imposed temporary wage and price ceilings because inflation in the previous year had reached the unsettling rate of almost 6 percent. The OPEC oil embargoes of 1973 and 1979 added two oil shocks to the already upwardly moving price level, bringing double-digit inflation into our lives.

Inflation came to a climax—and our present troubles began—in the closing months of 1979. Following the powerful lead of Chairman Paul Volcker, the Board of Governors of the Federal Reserve system decided that the situation was getting out of hand. Rightly or wrongly— there are arguments on both sides—the Federal Reserve slammed the brakes on the expansion of money and credit. As banks scrambled for funds, interest rates went through the roof. The prime rate and the rate on short-term business credit went to over 20 percent in 1981, when credit was available at all.

It is not surprising that such money rates imposed a great deal of suffering. Major nations like Mexico and Brazil flirted with bankruptcy, major financial institutions teetered on the brink of failure, and small-firm bankruptcies grew to epidemic size. Big businesses reined in their expenditures. Unemployment rose from 6 million in 1979 to 12 million by the end of 1982, a rise that was not deliberately planned or explicitly sought by the Federal Reserve, but that provided the active ingredient in the medicine it applied. Thus began the 1981–82 recession/depression, the worst "bad times" since the Great Depression—although, in sharp contrast to that earlier period, these bad times had been purposefully engineered rather than falling from the blue.

We now reach the part of the story that concerns us. With the near-depression came a swelling of the federal government's deficit. It swelled because government's tax receipts fell off, as they always do when business is bad, and because government expenditures increased, as *they* always do in slow times—some outlays, such as loans to hard-up farmers or payments for unemployment relief or welfare, are geared to economic distress. Hence the budget deficit rose from $40 billion in fiscal 1979 to $128 billion in fiscal 1982. Most businessmen, bankers, politicians, and economists applauded this rise as evidence that the "automatic stabilizing mechanisms" were at work, cushioning the slump.

What happened next took everyone by surprise. By 1982 the rate of inflation had fallen from 9.7 to 6.4 percent, and the next year it fell further to 3.9 percent. At the same time, real gross national product, which had dropped by 2.5 percent in 1982, rebounded to a vigorous 3.6 percent increase in 1983. *But instead of moving toward balance, the deficit rose to $208 billion.*

In 1984, the growth of GNP burst all bounds and inflation went down even further, but the deficit declined only to $185 billion. The next year was worse: GNP continued to rise—not so dramatically as in 1984, but enough to bring unemployment down for the second year in a row—and inflation declined to a mere 3 percent. The deficit, however, hit a new high of $212 billion. In 1986, income continued to grow and inflation continued to fall, but the deficit went still higher, to an unprecedented $221 billion. The years 1987 and 1988 were more of the same: growing GNP, with a hint of prices turning upward again, and continued disappointing performance with the federal deficit—$150 billion in fiscal 1987, 155 billion in fiscal 1988. This is where we stand now.

Why did everything go awry?

Most people believe that we ended up with the deficit problem because the Reagan administration made a fatal error by cutting income taxes at the same time that it undertook an enormous buildup of our defense establishment. Certainly both the tax cut and defense policy contributed to the deficit, but we would be seriously oversimplifying the problem if we laid the full blame on tax cuts and defense alone. For even as the administration pressed for higher levels of defense spending, it proposed cutbacks in nondefense outlays. However painful or ill-advised these cuts may have been, they substantially offset the growth in military spending.

Shortly thereafter, increases in payroll taxes, mandated to restore solvency to the Social Security system, more than offset the reductions in income tax revenues. Thus, rhetoric to the contrary notwithstanding, the Reagan administration did not cut taxes. It merely shifted them from individual (and corporate) payers to payroll payers. As a percentage of gross national product, total revenues averaged *a little higher* during the Reagan years than during the eight years prior to it.

Why then did the deficit so stubbornly refuse to shrink, once the economy recovered its stride in 1982? The answer lies in three factors quite unforeseen by Reagan administration economists or, for that matter, by economists anywhere.

The first of these factors was another legacy of the inflation that was rampant as the administration came in: the high level of entitlements like Social Security and Medicare payments. The cost of living had risen by 13 percent during 1979, 12 percent during 1980, and by 9 percent in 1981. These alarming increases—themselves the cause for the Federal Reserve's determination to bring inflation to a halt at all costs—had one effect that was unplanned and uncontrollable. The Social Security and Medicare payments received by approximately 37 million people jumped sharply upward, because these payments were "indexed" to the cost of living.

As the cost of living rose, so did disbursements. During 1979–1981, the administration faced an entitlement bill that was nearly $400 billion higher than it would have been had the increase in the cost of living remained at the average rate of the 1973–1980 period.[2] This was a substantial cause of the deficit—a cause that the Reagan administration did not create by its tax or spending policies, but simply inherited from the actions of previous administrations and Congresses.

The second factor was the effect on tax revenues of the end of inflation. The spiral of inflation came to an abrupt halt after 1981. The following year, the cost of living rose by only 4 percent. This slowed down the *rise* in entitlement payments, but total entitlement disbursements continued to grow. Meanwhile, the drop in inflation played havoc with tax receipts. Despite the jump in real output, tax receipts actually fell from $618 billion in 1982 to $600 billion in 1983. And although revenues rose thereafter, total tax income never achieved the level expected by administration economists, who thought that inflation would continue to boost incomes (and tax liabilities) throughout the 1980s as it had during the 1970s.

The third and most difficult problem was interest on the national debt. When the debt was growing most rapidly, during the years from 1981 to 1983, interest rates were still very high. As a result, the government's bill for interest began to rise very rapidly. Interest payments on the publicly held national debt in 1980 were $53.3 billion. By 1982 they were $85 billion. They surpassed $100 billion in 1984 and rose every year thereafter. By 1986 the average interest rate paid by the government was over nine percent, more than double its interest rate in the 1960s; and interest on the national debt had become the fastest growing major item in the budget.

Thus the problem turned into a case of the dog chasing its tail. As government borrowed to counteract the recession of the early 1980s, it had to pay the high interest rates that were holdovers from the inflation era; and the more it had to borrow at high rates, the larger its interest obligations became. Meanwhile, the larger its interest obligations, the more the Treasury had to borrow in the face of disappointing tax revenues. All this was certainly made more difficult because the administration had slashed tax rates on incomes and had tilted government spending upwards because of its defense ambitions. But even in the absence of tax cuts or any military buildup, we would still have faced the extraordinary problem of an exploding deficit because of inflation-swollen entitlements, inflation-boosted interest rates, and post-inflation reduced tax revenues.

The deficit explosion was thus an unexpected—and very unwelcome—consequence of anti-inflation policy. There is no use asking whether there might not have been some milder and equally effective way of bringing inflation under control. Perhaps if there is a "next time" we will do better. But when Paul Volcker tells us that the deficit is our number-one problem, he should know. It was the success of his policies that gave much of the deficit to us.

3

A First Look at the National Debt

WE HAVE COME to understand why the deficit question has suddenly exploded on us; we are ready to move on to the question of what this explosion entails for our well-being. But we cannot proceed until we have determined more precisely what debts and deficits are. Debts are household words, but we will quickly discover that even they have unfamiliar economic implications. Deficits are certainly not household words. Both terms deserve exploration.

Let us start with debt. A debt is a legal claim that someone holds against someone else. The claim may be of many kinds: IOUs, loan agreements, bonds of various sorts. The national debt is the sum total of all the outstanding bonds, bills, and notes issued by the Treasury to individuals and institutions who have lent the government their money.* As of the end of fiscal 1988, the estimated federal gross

---

*What is the the difference among these obligations? A bill is a debt with a short maturity—usually 30, 60, or 90 days. A note is an obligation that comes due in a year. A bond has a longer maturity, up to 30 years. The British exchequer used to issue "consols"—bonds in perpetuity. They were much prized by British investors.

debt totaled $2,600,700,000,000—or roughly $10,000 for every man, woman, and child in the nation.

To whom does the U.S. government owe this debt? Table 1 lists its principal creditors. Four points stand out in this first overview. The first is how surprisingly small is the portion of the debt directly owned by individuals— about seven percent of the total. We tend to think of the debt as owed to (and owned by) families. Instead, we find it mostly owed to and owned by institutions, public and private. Many of these institutions, such as banks or insurance companies, provide services such as checking accounts or various kinds of coverage whose costs are paid for, at least in part, by the interest received from their holdings of government debt. The fact remains that individuals, as we think of them, own only a small fraction of the outstanding Treasury obligations.

Second, note that a substantial share of the total debt is held by the government itself! We shall have more to say

Table 1. Who Owns the National Debt? Gross Public Debt of the U.S. Treasury by Holder, June 30, 1988

	$ billions	*% of total*
U.S. government agencies and trust funds	534.2	21.0
Federal Reserve banks	227.6	8.9
Commercial banks	263.0	10.3
Money market funds	13.4	0.5
Financial institutions	715.8	28.1
State and local treasuries	280.2	11.0
Individuals: Savings bonds	106.2	4.2
Marketable issues	75.0	2.9
Foreign and international	332.3	13.0
Total gross debt	2547.7	100.0

Source: Federal Reserve *Bulletin,* December 1988.

about this curious fact below. Third, note also that 13 percent of the total national debt is owned by foreigners, including central banks, ordinary foreign banks, foreign companies, institutions, and individuals. Many people worry about the power this may give to foreigners. We must remember that holders of bonds do not have voting rights of any sort. They can, of course, sell their bonds as a vote of "no confidence," and that may have effects on our bond market, on interest rates, or on the international value of the dollar. Foreign central banks who own substantial quantities of Treasury bonds—for example, the Bank of England, the Bank of Japan, or the German Bundesbank—may also urge various policies on the American government. But such admonitions are not just the prerogative of debt holders. The United States frequently urges other governments to change their positions on various matters, whether the Federal Reserve banks hold their debts or not. Owning a fraction of a nation's debt does not convey any special leverage to the holder; it may, in fact, make the creditor a hostage to the debtor's fortunes.

In Chapter X we shall look into some of these international problems. But we add here a word directed at the fright associated with the specter of a mass flight from American bonds and other assets. "It is a mystery to me," writes Nobelist Milton Friedman, "why . . . it is regarded as a sign of Japanese strength and American weakness that the Japanese find it more attractive to invest in the U.S. than Japan. Surely it is precisely the reverse—a sign of U.S. strength and Japanese weakness."[3]

Then there is the final point, brought home when we look at who owns the debt. It is the perhaps surprising realization that national debts serve a very useful purpose:

to provide a unique IOU with the full faith and credit of the government behind it. We often forget that government bonds are the only securities that carry such a guarantee of repayment. No state, locality, or corporation can match this guarantee because none of them possesses the powers that put all national governments in a class by themselves—the power to tax their national citizenry (not just the residents of a city or state) and the power to create money. Investors, foreign or national, buy government bonds to do themselves a favor, not out of motives of patriotism (wartime excepted) or in the expectation of exerting some sort of influence over the government—their own or someone else's.

If we did not have such a gilt-edged debt, we would dearly miss it. Where else would we invest all, or at least a very substantial fraction, of the mounting surpluses that the Social Security Trust Fund is expected to accumulate over the next decades? What other kinds of paper have sufficient liquidity—or are politically appropriate—for the Federal Reserve to buy and sell as part of its weekly multi-billion-dollar adjustment of the nation's money supply? Where would pension funds, insurance companies, corporations, and households place that fraction of their financial assets that they wish to keep as core reserves?

There is a curious aspect to these "ultimate powers" that put the debts of national governments in a class by themselves: the powers are ultimate only to the extent that the government does not use them. The power to tax is what makes the owners of government debt more certain that their interest checks will arrive than the owners of any other kind of debt—and yet, as we all know, the power to tax is also the power to destroy. The power to create currency, which every sovereign government has, cherishes, and uses when needed, also lends its vast weight to the value of government obligations, but the power to create currency is also the power to debase it, the road to many a country's ruin.

This suggests that we must consider features other than those of ultimate, but largely unused powers, in appraising the meaning of a national debt. A debt taken on to buy a house or to pay for a home computer has a justification that is completely lacking in a debt contracted to cover gambling losses. The former has an asset behind it; the latter does not. In the same way, a loan taken out by a company to buy new machinery is in a different class from one incurred to meet its normal payroll.

In the American economy as a whole, assets tower over debts. As of mid-1988, outstanding mortgages on family dwellings came to over $2.1 trillion, but the value of residential housing was about $5.0 trillion. Consumers owed $280 billion on automobile loans, but the value of their automobiles was $1.5 trillion. On top of that were financial assets owned by households, bank accounts, stocks and bonds, insurance and pension reserves, which added up to almost $10 trillion.[4] Among these assets, one that catches our attention is the previously noted $180 billion worth of Treasury obligations owned by households—that is, $180 billion worth of the national debt.

And so it should come as no surprise that the national debt is also backed by assets. Back in 1986, when the value of all Treasury obligations totaled $2.2 trillion, the value of the assets owned by the federal government came to $3.9 trillion.[5] This includes structures such as federal office buildings, post offices, NASA equipment, the value of military hardware, gold, the national parks, and a host of other assets. Some of these assets, such as federally owned land or reserves of oil, gas, and coal, are valued far below market value. Gold holdings, for some obscure reason, are valued at $42 per ounce, only one-eighth of their market value.

Taking the official estimate at its face value, however, the government's net worth—the difference between the official valuation of its assets and its debt liabilities—is clearly much smaller than that of households or corporations. Indeed, by the end of 1988, when the value of all Treasury obligations amounted to $2.6 trillion, the net worth of the federal government was probably close to zero; and looking ahead to 1990, when the debt is sure to climb over the $3 trillion level, the government's net worth will be negative unless we revalue our public holdings of federal resources by a great deal in the meantime.

Is it worrisome that the federal government's real assets may not be worth more than its liabilities?* The question brings to a proper conclusion this first look at the govern-

---

*A sharp-eyed reader will note that the value of all government obligations—the gross federal debt—is $2.6 billion, considerably larger than the debt held by the public, $2.1 billion. We will explain the difference in Chapter 7. We ought also to call attention to the fact that there are many ways of estimating the net value of government assets. According to the calculations of Robert Eisner and Paul Pieper, the government's net worth was already slightly negative in 1984. According to the calculations of Michael J. Boskin, Marc S. Robinson, John M. Roberts, and various collaborators, it was not. There is more than one way of evaluating many government assets, such as land, military equipment, and the like. We have to consider this problem again when we come to "measure" the deficit. See Robert Eisner, *How Real Is the Federal Deficit?* Free Press, New York, 1986, Table 3.3, and ch. 3, fn. 2.

ment debt. For it forces us to recognize that there is no accurate monetary value that can be applied to the wealth of a nation-state. In part this is because no one can put a dollar value on its sheer geography—its mountains and rivers, shorelines and plains. In part it is also because there are some things, such as national sovereignty, that money cannot buy. The value of the tangible assets owned by the government, even if we could calculate it, is irrelevant.

Then what is the "real" asset behind the national debt? Is it the equivalent of the house behind the mortgage and the machinery behind the bank loan? Not exactly. The asset behind the national debt is the national economy—all of its land, mines, factories, and buildings, its immense store of knowledge, and not least its skilled and educated workforce. God only knows what the monetary value of this economy is, but it is enormously greater than the total money value of the Treasury's bonds. It would be a fortunate bank that held a mortgage on the United States for a mere $2.6 trillion. The bond holders who own the national debt do not have to fear for the safety of their investment.

4

Is the Debt Too Big?

THE FACT THAT a national debt is really backed by a national economy gives us a way of reducing its awesome presence to comprehensible size. The way to appraise the safety of our debt is to compare it with the income generated by our economy.

This is the usual way that lenders appraise all debts. Here is John Doe applying for a $100,000 loan. The bank inquires into his assets and is told that they are few. The applicant has a fancy apartment, but it is a rental, not a co-op. He drives a Rolls Royce, but it too is leased. He has a normal bank account but no stocks and bonds. Judging by his assets, our applicant will never get his loan. But he has one thing going for him. He has an annual income of $500,000 from a trust fund that cannot be touched, although the trust sends him a check for $125,000 every quarter. Does our applicant get the loan? He does.

Thus assets are not essential to establish the credit worthiness of a borrower. The borrower's income is just as important, if not more so, because income, even more than assets, assures the lender that the borrower will be able to pay the interest and amortization of the loan as they come due.

Once again, there is a useful analogy to the national debt. The gross national product is a rough measure of the income of a nation, because it totes up the sales value of the annual production of the national economy. GNP is the equivalent of the trust fund that pays our imaginary applicant his income. It therefore becomes the basis for appraising the security of national debts because it shows us the flow of total income from which the government can derive its normal revenues.

In Table 2 we see how large the U.S. debt looks on this basis. What we see may come as something of a surprise. The national debt was a considerably larger proportion of our GNP in the 1950s and 1960s than it is today. Actually, in 1952 the ratio of debt to GNP had already greatly declined from its war-swollen level of 1945, when the net debt of the government was bigger by ten percent than total GNP. Perhaps we should recall that all during those halcyon years we had no trade deficit, imperceptible infla-

Table 2. Federal Debt Held by the Public as a Percentage of GNP

Year	Federal debt	GNP ($ billions)	Debt as % of GNP
1952	215	342	63
1962	248	557	45
1972	322	1153	28
1982	919	3139	29
1984	1300	3688	35
1986	1888	4187	41
1987	1828	4434	43
1988	2050	4750	43

Source: Economic Report of the President, 1989.

tion, and moderate interest rates, although the debt was a much larger proportion of GNP than it is today.

Table 2 makes clear as well the problem we looked at in Chapter II: the steep and sudden rise in the ratio of debt to GNP since 1982. Despite this rise, if we divide the national debt in 1986—the worst of the "explosion" years— by that year's GNP, we get a ratio of debt to GNP that is nearly fifty percent *smaller* than that of 1952 and no larger than that of 1962.

Thus, judging by its relation to income, our present level of debt is in no way remarkable. We have had larger debt ratios, without adverse consequences. We may well have them again. To quote Milton Friedman once more:

The size of the deficit has been exaggerated by use of such adjectives as "tremendous," "gigantic," "obscene." As a percentage of the national income, the deficit is not out of line with levels frequently reached in the past. Indeed . . . , the combined government deficit is considerably lower than in many past year and lower than in Japan, West Germany, and France—whose pundits have been among the loudest in decrying the U.S. deficit.[6]

Friedman's point about other nations is well taken. Table 3 compares the ratio of net general government debt (including state and local) to GNP among the major industrial nations in 1980 and in 1986, the latest year for which detailed figures are available. The table ranks these countries in descending order, based on the relative growth in the public debt over this period of time.

This table shows the United States' performance in a relatively favorable light. Our public debt-to-income ratio is in the middle range of these industrial nations. In addition, the growth in our public debt has been modest com-

Table 3. General Government Net Debt as Percent of GNP[a]

	1980	1986	% change
Canada	11.6	23.7	104.30
France	9.1	18.2	100.0
Italy	61.8	99.2	60.5
West Germany	14.4	22.1	53.5
Japan	17.3	26.3	52.0
United States	19.8	28.7	46.0
United Kingdom	48.1	46.5	−3.3

Source: Nouriel Roubini and Jeffrey Sachs, *Political and Economic Determinants of Budget Deficits in the Industrial Democracies,* National Bureau of Economic Research Working Paper #2682, Table 3.
[a]See footnote on page 79.

pared to what has happened in five out of the other six countries.

All this is not to deny that our debt may become a problem if other aspects of our national performance do not improve—for example, if our import surplus remains too large or if our real growth rate lags.

But it is useful to begin by demolishing frights. One of them is that the United States has been running up its public debt in profligate fashion while the rest of the industrial world has been conducting its fiscal affairs in abstemious rectitude. We can see that this is not so.

5

The Burden of the Debt

COMPARING debt and GNP brings us to the burden that debts impose on their national communities. That burden is the cost of having a debt, and that cost, in turn, assumes two forms. One is the interest payments the debt imposes. The other is the cost of paying the debt back.

Let us start with interest payments. More precisely let us begin by comparing the size of these payments to GNP and to the government's tax revenues, just as a banker would compare interest to an applicant's total income and to his personal budget. We make these comparisons in Table 4.

Interest payments have certainly gone up strikingly in dollar amounts, tripling over the last decade. They have gone up much less sharply when compared to GNP because gross national product itself almost doubled over the period.

By one standard of conventional banking, then, the burdensomeness of the interest cost has grown slightly but is still a very modest proportion of the nation's income. Even in 1988, when interest payments reached an all-time high,

**Table 4. GNP, Tax Revenues, and Interest Costs
on Publicly Held Debt**

Fiscal years	GNP	Tax revenue	Interest	Tax revenue	Interest
		($ billions)		(as % of GNP)	
1980	2671	517.1	50.8	19.4	1.9
1981	2986	599.3	66.7	20.1	2.2
1982	3139	617.8	82.2	19.7	2.7
1983	3322	600.6	90.6	18.1	2.7
1984	3687	666.5	109.7	18.1	3.0
1985	3952	734.1	125.3	18.6	3.2
1986	4187	769.1	134.4	18.4	3.2
1987	4434	854.1	139.7	19.3	3.2
1988	4780	909.0	150.4	19.0	3.1

Source: Economic Report of the President, 1989.

they were covered more than six times over by tax revenues. Moreover, the "trust fund" of the U.S.'s gross national product, from which tax revenues arise, has grown steadily, more or less at the same rate as the GNPs of its major competitors, the extraordinary record of Japan excepted. *As long as growth continues and the debt remains in the same relation to GNP, there is no reason that a national debt cannot increase indefinitely.* *

On the other hand, a banker would not be pleased to learn that his client was spending more and more of his trust fund income on paying interest. Understandably, economists are not pleased that interest costs, which used to be negligible, are today larger than the deficit.

*To be sure, the fact that a nation's gross national product is growing is no ironclad guarantee that its government's income is also growing: let us not forget that in 1981 we passed the largest tax reduction act in our history. Yet, as we noted in Chapter 2, tax revenues have kept pace with GNP despite these reductions. From 1986 through 1988, tax revenues averaged 18.9 percent of GNP, a percentage point below the early 1980s. What had been lost in individual and corporate taxes was made up in Social Security taxes and economic growth.

Let us therefore look at these interest payments more carefully. We immediately notice one thing about them, whose basis lies in a matter we examined in the previous chapter. Most interest payments go to American households or institutions. They therefore remain within the great flow of incomes from which the government gets its own revenues, whether through taxes or through borrowing. The fact that 87 percent of all interest (as of mid-1988) remained within the reach of government makes our debt largely "internal," not "external." The difference between an internal and an external debt is the difference between owing money to a bank and owing it to your own mother-in-law. That is why a national government's debt is always safer than that of a city or a state. Texas knows that its bonds are as likely to be owned by Californians as by Texans, so there is no assurance that it can "recapture" the interest payments it makes by taxing Texans' incomes. *But the United States knows that 87 percent of the interest payments on its bonds will indeed remain within its taxing authority, available for financing the government, if need be.* *

Second, we ought to note that interest is not a burden for all taxpayers. Specifically, it is not a burden for those

---

*The internality of the national debt is by all odds the characteristic that distinguishes it most decisively from all other kinds of debt. It is sometimes said, half cynically, that national debts do not matter because "we owe them to ourselves." National debts *do* matter, but it is true nonetheless that we owe them to ourselves, at least to the extent that they are owned by citizens who remain within the taxing reach of government. Therefore they matter less than they would if they were owned by noncitizens from whom there was no way of recouping, by taxation, some part of the interest they received on their holdings of the debt. Compare the situation of the United States, whose externally held debt in mid-1988 was 13 percent of its gross national product, to that of Costa Rica, whose external debt is as large as its GNP. And there are worse cases than Costa Rica.

who receive more income in the form of Treasury interest checks than they contribute (buried in their tax bill) to the government's interest payments. Although it is much more difficult to calculate, the interest on the national debt is also not all burden for those who benefit indirectly from Treasury interest payments that defray part of the banking costs that depositors would otherwise have to shoulder, or who benefit from interest on government bonds paid to pension funds or other such institutions.

The burden of interest costs thus varies from one family to the next. For some it is a net gain; for others a net loss. We know, however, that households with assets worth a half million dollars or more own about 20 percent of federal bonds, and that the average American family owns no government bonds directly. It seems fair to say, therefore, that the government debt is a net expense for the lower three-quarters of the nation, and a net benefit for the upper one-quarter. Thus one very real but largely overlooked aspect of the interest burden lies in its impact on the distribution of income. Obviously, the more widely held the debt, the less the burden will fall on those in the lower- and middle-income groups.[7]

Now for the matter of paying the debt back. When we speak of the immense burden of the debt, don't we mean the huge cost imposed when the debt becomes due and the Treasury sends out its bills asking us to wipe the slate clean? If the debt is $3 trillion when the fateful day comes, and the number of households 100 million, each American family will owe $30,000. Most American families do not have that much money or could raise it only by selling their houses, cashing in their insurance, or surrendering all their liquid assets. What then?

There are only two answers to this terrible problem. One of them is that in one way or another the dreaded sale takes place, and 100,000,000 families find buyers for their homes, cars, stocks, bonds, insurance, and collectibles. Whatever the means, the end result must be that all the Treasury's bills, notes, and bonds will have been redeemed and the national debt therefore paid back. Those who proffered their bonds for payment will have been sent checks by the government and may have bulging bank accounts. Those who paid their tax bills, but did not receive checks because they had no bonds, will have been reduced to penury. Paying back the debt, in other words, means a transfer of assets on a gargantuan scale from those who have not to those who have. *Our society will be neither richer nor poorer, only more unhappy.* More important, our real productive wealth—our factories and utility lines and houses and schools and roads—will remain unchanged as a result of this financial saturnalia.

Seen from this viewpoint, the charge that the government deficit is somehow leaving a shocking burden to the next generation rings totally false. With the exception of the portion owed to foreigners, the same generation that would pay off the debt will be receiving the proceeds of the redemption. The next generation will be neither worse off nor better off than it would have been to begin with.

There is, however, an alternative: not to pay back the debt. Of course, each and every bill, note, and bond will have to be honored when its due date comes around, by sending its owner a check for the exact amount owing. All debts, public as well as private, carry this obligation. But the repayment of each individual bond does not preclude the issuance of another bond from whose proceeds the first is redeemed. Indeed, this is precisely what happens every week in the market for all bonds, private and public.

Again we use the household sector to illustrate the point. Every home mortgage must eventually be paid, usually in installments—amortization. But the sum total of all household mortgages is not repaid. As one householder pays off the last of his mortgage with a sigh of relief, another takes on a fresh mortgage for a house that has just been built. With corporations, it is a little easier. As each company's issue of bonds comes due, it may pay back its bond holders from its cash reserves, just as the mortgagor repays the bank, over time, from his savings. Or the corporation may, and often does, simply issue new bonds to pay off the old.

As a result, although each and every mortgage is paid off, excepting occasional defaults leading to foreclosures, the sum total of mortgages grows over time. In 1970, home mortgage debt was $279 billion, a mere one-seventh of the 1988 total. The numbers get larger not merely because of inflation, but also because the number of homes is growing. Corporate debt shows the same trend: $363 billion in 1970, almost $2 trillion in 1988. Not only are corporate debts as a whole never paid off, as new issues "re-fund" the old or add to their total value, but the debts of *individual* large companies are also often never paid off. IBM, to take a typical example, owed $173 million in long-term debt in 1960, $4.5 billion in 1988; Exxon's debt rose nine-fold over the same period.

Thus the debts of the *sectors* of the economy—households as a whole, businesses as a whole, the states and localities as a whole, and the federal government, which *is* a whole—are never paid off in a growing economy, even though each bond and note is fully discharged. As long as total output grows, debts also steadily grow and should grow, because they serve a purpose that is integrally connected with growth.

Is there, then, *no* burden to a debt? The question has to be answered carefully. If debt remains a steady fraction of GNP, we should experience no burden because tax revenues would provide the needed interest. If debt gets larger, it should still pose no burden as long as the economy grows fast enough to provide the additional tax revenues needed for additional interest. The payments of interest, in turn, should not burden an economy if they do not impose a large flow of income to foreign holders of our debt or if they do not impose severe distortions in the way income is divided. Finally, the complications imposed by the repayment of debt vanish if the government, like the corporate or household sectors, does not seek to repay its debt but only to renew it.

Note that all these reassurances are preceded with ifs. That poses the question as to whether our economic situation at the moment threatens to cross over the danger lines that these ifs mark out.

We are not ready to answer these questions, except for the last: no one should lose any sleep over the burden associated with paying the debt back. The other questions will be examined in due course. But surely the reader can already anticipate the theme that will run through all the answers. The burden of the debt will hinge on matters largely independent of the debt itself—the modernization of our productive structure, the evolution of the world economy, the intelligence of our tax and expenditure programs. Will the debt and the deficit interfere with our capacity to make these changes? We shall see. But provided that these problems can be dealt with well enough, the debt should not be a burden. Indeed, as we shall see in our next chapter, it may even be part of the solution.

6

The Uses of Debt

WHY DO national debts exist in the first place?

The question is not often asked, and its answer will further clarify our thinking.

All debts exist because borrowers want funds that they do not immediately possess. Governments are no exception. A government that seeks to borrow does so because its tax revenues are not sufficient to finance all the expenditures that it has budgeted.

Why not raise taxes? The main reason is that taxing is often a politically unpopular, or even socially disruptive, means of raising money. Even under wartime conditions, when the appeal of patriotism is at its height, there are limits to how far the government can go in taxing the incomes of its citizens. During World War II, for example, the tax paid by families in the top income bracket was "only" 90 percent of their income over $1 million.

Taxes reach their limit when the incentive to conceal income or to cheat on or evade taxes begins to override the promptings of patriotism. In the United States, as elsewhere, the costs of World War II were financed by borrowing as well as by taxes. For the entire five years of the war, the government spent a total of $324 billion, or forty percent of the gross national product, and raised only $211 billion by taxation. That is why we found ourselves at the end of the war with a national debt that exceeded the total GNP.

Although the desire to avoid social friction probably applies with greatest force during periods of unusual government demands for funds such as wartime, the question of social friction is always present to some degree when a government decides to borrow instead of raising taxes. From the economist's point of view, however, there is a second reason that is unrelated to social pressures. Governments may borrow rather than tax because it is economically sensible and rational to do so, exactly as is the case with households or corporations.

The main circumstance in which borrowing is rational is when a borrower seeks to raise capital. Capital itself is an elusive word. In daily usage, capital often refers to personal wealth, such as stocks and bonds. This is not, however, the meaning that mainly interests economists. Machines, industrial or commercial plant, equipment, and the like are capital to the economist, because they make society more productive. From this point of view, the stocks or bonds that constitute our personal capital appear not as embodiments of real wealth but as the personal *claims* to that real wealth.

Moreover, because economists are interested in capital as the means by which economic growth is enhanced, they use the word to denote some expenditures that we ordinarily think of as consumption spending—spending devoted to personal enjoyments. Household outlays on education, for instance, not only increase personal learning, which is an enjoyment, but very likely contribute to productivity as we become more skilled and knowledgeable at work. The economist therefore regards at least some part of education expenditure as building up "human capital"—a form of wealth every bit as important as, and maybe in the long run much more important than, physical capital as a source of economic growth.

Here is the first constructive purpose of debt. *Borrowing can play a useful role in the creation of physical and human capital.* Borrowing enables us to pay over time for capital assets that we need now but that cost more money than we can immediately raise. Even the richest corporation would have trouble paying for a billion-dollar expansion program all in cash up front. Moreover, the rational consideration—not just the practical one—behind such a deferred payment is that the capital we acquire, whether in the form of a machine, a physical structure, or an education, will usually yield its benefits over a number of years into the future, whereas consumption expenditure typically yields its benefits very quickly. Hence it makes sense to go into serious debt for a medical education, but not for a cruise.

Does government also finance capital building programs by borrowing? Yes and no. The yes is that the same rationale applies to government borrowing to build a road as business borrowing to build a plant. As economist Benjamin Friedman writes, "to the extent that part of what the government spends goes for physical investments, like office buildings or interstate highways or military installations, financing such expenditures by borrowing is no more than what any business putting up a new plant typically does—or any family building a new house."[8] The no is that the government does not keep its books the way business does, with important and surprising results that we shall shortly come to.

First, however, we need to look further into the yes part of the answer. There is a manifest similarity between the capital-building activities of the private and public sectors, although the private sector, as we would expect, is much larger than the public. In 1988, private business spent about $750 billion to expand or restore its real capital, whereas the government, according to the Office of Management and Budget, spent for fiscal 1988 about $200 billion for similar purposes.

Both figures, we ought to note, are a jumble of things, some a good deal more growth promoting than others. Private capital expenditure includes building or renovating office buildings and amusement parks as well as investing in state-of-the-art machinery and high-tech ventures. Their differing encouragement to growth aside, some of these ventures will pay off in profits; others will not.

Much the same higgledy-piggledy character applies to government investment. The government's officially designated "growth-related" spending is a conglomeration of undertakings that range from adding to or maintaining its military equipment to fixing up post office buildings and launching space exploration. As with the private sector, some of these undertakings will boost the nation's growth and some may even retard it, but unlike the private sector, none will make or lose money. The government is not in the business of business. Finally, it is important to note that there are some public and some private expenditures that are counted as consumption but that ought to be included in investment because they certainly promote production: not only education but medical expenses that restore us to working health.

The sorting out of both private and public expenditures that clearly enhance economic growth will become a matter of some importance when we discuss the relationship of government budgets to national economic performance. But what is critical at the moment is a much simpler idea—that the public sphere, like the private, makes a contribution to economic growth. Furthermore, despite its small size relative to private capital spending, public investment makes a vital contribution. Without an adequate infrastructure—an efficient transportation system, for example—private industry cannot work up to its own potential. One of the distressing aspects of our present economic situation is that, despite our exploding debt, total government spending for infrastructure and education (state and local as well as federal) has not been expanding to keep pace with gross national product.

A study by David Aschauer of the Chicago Federal Reserve bank concludes that the productivity of public investment today exceeds that of private investment. Indeed, the costs imposed on the private sector by an inadequate infrastructure are so great that private profitability would rise by two percentage points if nondefense public investment were to rise from its present abysmal low of 0.3 percent of GNP to the 2.1 percent level of the early 1980s.* Anyone who has blown a tire on a poorly main-

---

*See also *The Economic Report of the President,* 1989, pp. 80–81.

tained road can understand what these costs are. And even 2.1 percent is nothing to brag about. All our major industrial competitors spend much more than that on public investment: Japan, for example, invests about 5 percent of its output in public capital of various kinds. The well-maintained superhighways and bridges, "bullet train" rail transport, clean streets, and public amenities that strike every American visitor did not fall from the heavens. They were bought and paid for by public investment, generally through borrowing.[9]

The striking similarity between the public and private sectors as sources of capital building now brings us to an even more striking dissimilarity. It concerns the no part of the answer to the question we raised before as to whether the federal government, like business, finances its capital outlays by borrowing.

The difference is that private borrowers are careful to separate their capital expenditures from current operating expenses. That is, they do not charge the entire cost of a new machine or an addition to plant in the year in which they acquire these assets. Rather, they spread the cost of new capital over its productive life, each year picking up a year's interest and depreciation or amortization as part of the operating budget. In this way private borrowers match their payments for the capital funds they have borrowed against the flow of benefits they derive from the capital.

No such budgetary procedure exists in the federal budget. Instead, all expenditures for whatever purpose—as durable as a dam or as ephemeral as a White House dinner party—are lumped together. Our federal budget, in other words, is both a current budget and a capital budget rolled into one.

This difference in accounting practices has enormous consequences in understanding the national debt and the deficit. Picture an imaginary company with the following income statement:

Money received		Money paid out	
Sales	$1,000,000,000	All operating expenses	$800,000,000
New debt issued	$500,000,000	Cost of new plant	$500,000,000

We see that the company's total expenditures come to $1.3 billion—$800 million for the costs of producing this year's sales plus $500 million for its new plant—whereas its total sales revenues brought in only $1 billion. Does our company therefore report an annual loss of $300 million to its shareholders? It most certainly does not. Its year end statement will show a profit of $200 million on sales *because its capital expenditures will not be charged against its current revenues.* The $500 million cost of the new plant will be carried as a capital expense, written off year by year as the wear and tear of the plant and the tax laws require.

Why do we not have a U.S. budget that designates certain expenditures as "capital" or "growth-related" just as we do in any company's statement of its activities? There are two reasons for this strange omission. The first is that the government does not run a profit-oriented operation. As we have seen, government assets are not priced at market value, nor are government services priced at levels calculated to yield a profit. Where user fees are charged, such as entrance fees to the national parks, they are modest. Lacking the discipline of the market, for better or worse, the government is under no need to separate out its current costs from its capital costs in order to show a profit on its ordinary activities.

A second reason lies in the genuine difficulties in making up a national capital budget. Do tanks and warships, which look like capital, actually promote growth? How much of the $30 to $40 billion spent on military-related research has peacetime usefulness? Or consider the military payroll itself. The armed forces advertise that young men and women entering the service will receive training in computer skills and office techniques (or simply in living habits) that will raise their employability when they leave the forces. Are these not also growth-promoting expenditures?

By ducking these questions Congress avoids difficult and messy decisions that it would be forced to make if the national government were run like a business. By so doing, however, Congress imposes on itself, as well as on the nation, a serious cost. By treating all spending, whether for infrastructure or for pomp and display, as a form of public "consumption," the government hides a crucially important criterion by which its spending ought to be judged. Worse yet, it omits from public discussion the one explanation for borrowing that is understandable to every home buyer, student, or business person. "If these accounting principles were adopted by your business," Walter Wriston, former chairman of Citicorp told a meeting of the Busienss Council in October 1988,

the SEC would doubtless bring charges of misrepresentation of fact. . . . [E]verything the federal government buys is expensed—a several-billion-dollar road system, the space shuttle, an extension to Yellowstone Park, or a ten cent pencil. The IRS might get a little upset if your business did this, but that's the way the federal budget works. . . . The familiar refrain that every family must balance its budget, so why shouldn't the government, has a nice ring to it, but no family I know of expenses its home. . . . All in all capital expenditures added up to 13.2 percent of total federal outlays, a not inconsiderable amount to expense, and if funded in a capital budget, would produce near balance in the operating budget.*

We will come back to bad bookkeeping and its consequences. But first we must attend to another purpose served by debt, in addition to financing capital expenditure. Governments often borrow to stimulate the economy. Debt creation is one of the ways in which we drive the business system. The householder who takes out a mortgage, the business that floats a loan, are putting to work money that the lenders were *not* using; had they been planning to make use of it, the money would not have been available to the borrower.

The same function is served when the government borrows and spends. Is there the slightest difference, from the viewpoint of creating jobs and incomes, between AT&T borrowing $1 billion for a new microwave network and the Treasury borrowing $1 billion for a new communication satellite? Between a real estate developer borrowing to build a cooperative apartment house and government borrowing to build a housing project? There is none.

But—and it is a very big "but"—borrowing will not drive the economy if the system is already operating at full capacity. In that case, additional stimulus spending by any sector—a burst of home building, plant expansion, or gov-

*Wriston, remarks at the Business Council.

ernment spending on roads—will only add to the demand for labor or plant capacity when neither idle workers nor idle plant are available. The result will be a stimulus—but a stimulus to inflation rather than to growth. The roads will get built, but only at the expense of houses or private capital, and only with the unwanted side effect of another push to the price level.

The inescapable choice imposed on a fully employed economy points up one of the real—not the imaginary, the false-alarm—problems that come with government finance. The government, because it is a government, bears a degree of responsibility for the economy that the private sector does not and cannot bear. War finance is a perfect example. Treasury borrowing is always inflationary in wartime, because we have no slack resources. But during wartime there is also a general consensus that war production comes first. Hence, we accept the inflation—and acquiesce in higher taxes to keep it under control—as part of the price to get the arms and the armies we need.

Things are not so simple in peacetime, when the will to fight inflation is less and ready agreement about priorities is lacking. Hence the decision as to whether government should borrow, even for the best purposes, is always made difficult by the related question as to whether additional government spending will speed up inflation. To be sure, additional private spending may also be inflationary, but the private sector is driven by self-interest and no company is likely to ask itself whether it should curtail its own borrowing and spending to lessen the pressure on prices around the nation.

The government *is* often faced with exactly that question, the answer to which is rarely black or white. The creation of government debt must therefore be undertaken from a different perspective than the creation of private debt. There is a political aspect to government borrowing that sets it aside from private borrowing. As we will see this plays a considerable role as we think our way through the deficit dilemma.

7

Measuring the Deficit

WE HAVE BEEN focusing largely on the debt, not the deficit. But undoubtedly the connection has become clear. The national debt consists of the outstanding obligations of the United States Treasury. The deficit is simply the amount by which the debt rises from one date to the next—the net amount the Treasury has borrowed. If we wanted to, we could call our present national publicly held debt of $2.1 trillion the deficit we have run up since 1776. Usually we apply the word only to a single year's operations. We speak of the deficit for fiscal 1988 as $162 billion because our publicly held national debt on September 30, 1988, was $162 billion larger than one year earlier.

It would seem therefore a simple matter to discover exactly how large the deficit is. We find, however, that measuring the deficit is an extremely elusive procedure. Calculated one way it is very big; calculated another way it is small, and in certain years it actually disappears. Therefore before taking up the problems the deficit brings, we must know how to appraise the size of the thing that worries us.

To measure the deficit we must discover how much the national debt has increased from one year to the next. But how big is that debt? There are, to begin, two debts: the gross debt and the net debt. The gross debt is the sum total of all outstanding Treasury obligations. The net debt—the publicly held debt—is that total minus the amount of debt held by the government itself.

This is not a small adjustment. In mid-1988 almost $534 billion worth of Treasury obligations were owned by agencies of the federal government, of which the most important is the Social Security Trust Fund. The holdings of Treasury bonds (or other federal obligations) by these agencies illustrate a point we have made before—that the debt serves a very useful purpose in providing gilt-edged securities in which the government itself can repose its funds.

Of these two debts, the one that interests us is the net debt, the publicly held debt—just as any household is more concerned about the sums it owes to other people or institutions than about sums that one member of the family owes to another member. The part of the debt owned by agencies of the federal government is not a burden of any kind—it would be called on Wall Street a "wash": whatever is paid out with one hand is taken in with the other.

As of the end of fiscal 1988 the estimated net debt amounted to 2,050 billion, a lot smaller than the gross debt of 2,601 billion. The distinction between the gross and net debt takes on a special significance today because of the startlingly rapid growth of the Social Security Trust Funds, in which the revenues of the Social Security system are deposited.

As the Social Security fund expands, all or the great bulk of it will probably be invested in Treasury obligations, if only because there is no way to resolve the problem of where else to invest it. If that is indeed the case, there is likely to be an expansion of the gross debt to accommodate the needs of the Trust Funds, estimated to grow to $12 trillion by the year 2033.

Next we have to consider whether we count increases in the *federal* debt, or in *all* government debt, before we decide how large the deficit really is. Here the difference arises because of the financial linkage between the federal government and state and local governments. The budgets of state and local governments, taken together, generally show a surplus—an excess of revenues over expenditures—largely as the consequence of the buildup of the reserves in their pension funds in recent years. During the 1970s, state and local budgets were in surplus by an amount averaging one-half the federal deficit! This ratio has fallen since, partly because the federal government gives less to the states and partly because federal deficits have risen so rapidly beginning in 1982.

Nonetheless, even in 1987, the surpluses of states and localities amounted to some $53 billion—enough to reduce the government's net deficit in that calendar year from an estimated $158 billion to $105 billion; for calendar 1988, the state and local surplus is estimated at $56 billion, lowering the total government deficit for the year to well below $100 billion.[10]

Why should the surpluses of state and local governments be subtracted from the net debt of the federal government? The government regularly makes expenditures called "grants in aid" to the states and localities. These grants are no small sum—in 1988 they exceeded $110 billion. The surpluses of states and localities must therefore be subtracted from the deficit of the federal government because those surpluses were made possible by the expenditures of the federal branch. If that adjustment is made, the federal deficits from 1978 to 1988, which aggregate to $1,355 billion, are reduced to $861 billion. This is an adjustment made by all serious students of the deficit, but it is often overlooked when the deficit is trotted out as a national problem.

Now we turn to a third adjustment, having to do with the effect of inflation in measuring the deficit. We are used to taking inflation into account in many kinds of calculations, but we fail to consider it when measuring the deficit. As the numbers are very large, the omission is very important.

The inflation effect measures the difference between the visible money price of things—their "nominal price"—and the "real price"—the money price corrected for inflation. We all know that a dollar isn't worth what a dollar used to be, as the common complaint goes. The point that concerns us is that this loss of value applies to debt as well as to tangible things. A bond that we redeem for its face value of $1000 has lost some of the purchasing power that $1000 represented when we lent the money five or ten years ago. Therefore all borrowers in inflationary times have the advantage of paying their debts back in cheaper dollars than they borrowed; and all creditors have the disadvantage of being repaid in dollars that are not worth as much as the dollars they loaned.*

How does this inflation factor apply to measuring the deficit? We must allow for the advantage enjoyed by the Treasury because of the steady creep of inflation. "The real deficit," writes Stephen Entin, formerly assistant Treasury secretary for economic policy, "is the change in the real value of the federal debt from one year to the next. To put the deficit in real terms, one has to adjust it for the effect of inflation on the outstanding national debt."[11] The impact of this "inflation tax" on bondholders depends, of course, on the rate of inflation. In 1988 the rate was 3.5 percent. That rate, applied to the 1987 net debt of $1.9 trillion is $66 billion—enough to cut the deficit in half!

This adjustment is so dramatic that we must take a moment to make certain that its application is entirely warranted. Suppose that we did not take the inflation out of the deficit. This would mean that the funds we lent to the government a year, five years, and in some cases up to

---

*The disadvantage that creditors suffer and the advantage that debtors gain is compensated, to some extent at least, by higher interest rates. A lender, knowing that he will be repaid in cheaper dollars, will not lend money unless the interest is high enough to make up for the expected loss in the real value of the bond—he asks for, let us say, 8 percent instead of 4 percent to compensate for an expected inflation rate of 4 percent. The borrower, aware that the bond will be redeemed in cheaper dollars, is willing to pay higher nominal interest rates, because after allowing for inflation the *real* cost of borrowing remains the same. Thus inflation raises the money price of borrowing, along with everything else, but it may not raise the real cost—that is, the cost of borrowing *compared* with the costs of everything else.

In fact this means that some of the interest on the national debt is not really interest at all, but a part repayment of capital that the borrower is forced to make to the lender. In inflationary times, the real interest cost to all borrowers is less than the nominal interest they pay. By way of confirmation of this unfamiliar proposition, we might note that British bonds geared to the cost of living—that is, inflation-free bonds—sell to yield an interest return of 3 percent. That is the "real" rate of interest. All the rest is merely a catch-up for inflation.

thirty years ago were not affected by the rise in prices we observe around us. In that case, the money we would receive from the government when our bonds came due would have as much purchasing power as it did five, ten, or thirty years ago! Government bonds would thereupon become what some people have urged that they should be: obligations indexed to the cost of living. If they were such cost-of-living bonds, however, we all know that the government would have to give us back *more* dollars than we loaned—not the same number of dollars—to "beat the inflation factor."

Thus, however dramatic and large it may be, an inflation adjustment must be applied to the national debt—or to any debt—just as it must be applied to the prices of houses, food, and anything else if we wish to see how much their real values have changed over time. Not unexpectedly, the effect of adjusting debt for inflation makes big numbers much smaller, and because the national debt is a very big number the adjustment is also very large. As Robert Eisner has pointed out, "With inflation we can have substantial budget deficits by the official measure while the true value of the net debt goes down." Eisner has shown, for example, that from 1945 to the end of 1980, the uncorrected value of the net federal debt rose from roughly $250 billion to almost $600 billion. With the inflation factor allowed for, the real value of the debt *fell* by almost 60 percent![12]

Finally, one last correction. Again and again we have referred to differences and similarities between public and private borrowing. One difference has especially warranted our attention: the private sector keeps its capital account separate from its current account, and the federal sector does not. Because of this difference, in accounting practices the federal sector runs a "deficit," but the private sector does not. As we have seen, the private sector's capital expenditures are not applied against its current income in the year they are made, but are charged off over the life of the capital goods.

If federal capital expenditures were handled the same way, we would add to our current budget each year some appropriate portion of our public capital expenditures, while keeping the unpaid portion in a special capital fund. The unpaid portion, financed by borrowing, would be carried as a liability of the government—the amount it owed its bond holders—exactly as are the outstanding bonds of any corporation and of many states and municipalities. And the net value of our public wealth would appear on the national balance sheet as an asset of the government, against which it had issued the liabilities of its bonds.

If we practiced this sort of rational bookkeeping, there could well be a shortfall in the current account if the government failed to generate enough taxes to pay for its ordinary expenses. And if the government borrowed to pay those bills, it would be quite proper to call that a deficit, comparable to the loss a company incurs when its normal expenses exceed its sales revenue. *But insofar as the borrowing was made to finance public capital, there would be no deficit, any more than a company would call its outstanding debt a deficit.*

Thus we have come to see that there are at least five sizes of the deficit based on five ways of measuring the government's debt:

(1) The gross deficit: the change in the total amount of Treasury debt issued during the year held by both the government itself and the public;

(2) the net deficit: the change in the gross debt less any debt held by federal agencies;

(3) the national—as opposed to federal—deficit: the change in the net debt less surpluses earned in the state and local sector;

(4) the inflation-adjusted deficit: the national deficit corrected for the loss of value of all federal obligations because of inflation;

(5) the operating deficit: the inflation-adjusted deficit corrected by setting aside the value of unwritten-off public capital formation.

Table 5 shows us these estimated amounts for fiscal 1988.

We reach the astonishing conclusion that the net, inflation-corrected, and public investment–corrected deficit was not $255 billion or even $162 billion. It was $3 billion. For all intents and purposes, there was no deficit.

This is so astonishing as to invite instant disbelief. Let us therefore run through the adjustments once more. There is little difficulty in explaining the reduction of the

**Table 5. Five Measures of the
Fiscal 1988 Deficit**

	($ billions)
Gross deficit	255
Net deficit	162
National deficit	109
Inflation adjusted deficit	43
Operating deficit	3

gross to the net deficit of $162 billion, the commonly cited measure of the deficit. The adjustment consists in setting aside the $93 billion of debt issued in 1988 that is held by the government itself. This is further reduced by the estimate of $53 billion of state and local surplus—a surplus that is attributable to the grants in aid of the federal government. This lowers the net debt from $162 billion to $109 billion.

Next we make a necessary correction for the decrease in the real value of the debt that results from inflation—precisely the same adjustment we would make if we were to calculate the real increase in GNP from one year to the next. This takes another $66 billion from the deficit, bringing the inflation-corrected figure down from $109 billion to $43 billion.

This remaining deficit is now almost eliminated by the estimated value of the government's net investment, discussed in the Appendix to this chapter. As can be seen there, these estimates are probably far too low.

Which is the correct measure of the deficit? There is no single correct measure.* The gross deficit shows us the rise in the value of all Treasury obligations; for financial pur-

---

*At the risk of hopeless confusion, let us add yet *another* method of calculating the debt, and therefore the deficit. In Table 3, page 44, the reader will note that the nomenclature for the debt is "general government net debt." This refers to a method used by the Organization for Economic Cooperation and Development. Debt is calculated by taking the publicly held liabilities of all government organizations (including states and localities) and subtracting their financial assets. This yields a smaller debt figure than the conventional U.S. method, which is why the ratio of debt to GNP in the table is less than in conventional U.S. statistics. The U.S. method would of course raise the ratios for all countries, not just for the United States. We add this note only to emphasize again how difficult it is to find a definitive measure of debts and deficits—and how important it is to be aware of the many legitimate ways of taking their measure.

poses this might be a useful figure. The net deficit shows us the increase in financial obligations owed by the Treasury to its American and foreign individual and institutional bond holders, an amount that is frequently compared with the size of GNP as a rough and ready indicator of the "true" size of the deficit. The net debt less other government surpluses is a better indicator of national, not federal, debt ratios, and certainly the figure by which we must compare the performance of the U.S. government with the governments of nations that do not have our kind of multilevel government. The row that adjusts these figures for inflation gives us an accurate measure of the real magnitude of the government's deficit, comparable to the real measure of its growth, which is also corrected for inflation.

And the last measure, which no one uses, would show us what the deficit looked like if we eliminated its capital-related portion. It is, in our judgment, the most rational form of the deficit. It is vastly smaller than the deficit (gross or net) as reported in conventional accounts. It is still the case, as we saw in Chapter II, that we have had a rapid increase in debt, but it must now be abundantly clear that today's deficit, *by any measure,* is far, far smaller than we think.

But has not the conventionally measured debt—the debt held by all individuals and institutions except the federal government itself—grown enormously, from $267 billion in 1960 to $2.1 trillion in 1988? Yes it has, but we can now see that the $1.8 trillion increase is a very unsatisfactory and imprecise measure of that growth. An explosion of debt has occurred, but it has been a muffled explosion. Its most revealing measure, as we have seen, is the ratio of debt to GNP. This has risen from a low 30 percent level, around which it hovered in the 1970s, to a low 40 percent level today—a very substantial rise, but not a volcanic event: compare the years from 1940 to 1945 when the debt-to-GNP ratio leaped from 43 percent to 110 percent.

Moreover, there is every reason to believe that the debt will remain around 40 percent of GNP, unless we drastically change our tax or expenditure policies or again attempt a Volcker-like squeeze on credit. None of these eventualities seems likely. Furthermore, this fraction, as we have seen, is entirely within our normal range of experience—note that the ratio is about where it was in 1940. As we have also seen, it is well within the range of other industrial nations. To worry about the present size of the debt is to magnify a mouse into a monster. It is simply a false alarm.

APPENDIX

Calculating the Net Growth-Related Expenditures of the Government

The budget of the United States is an immense document, thousands of pages long, in which matters of great consequence for the nation can be disposed of in a dependent clause. David Stockman rose to fame in the Reagan administration by virtue of his mastery of this vast repository of information; we have no doubt that he could compose this chapter more skillfully than we.

Our purpose is not, however, to perform an operation that would require an intimate acquaintance with the budget. We shall work only with the ready-to-hand *Budget of the United States Government, Special Analyses,* prepared annually by the Office of Management and Budget (OMB). In Table 6 we reproduce their Table D-1, which provides us with a first look at the "investment-type" and "growth-related" elements of six fiscal year budgets.

We have already mentioned some of the obvious problems with such budget breakdowns. A major difficulty involves the inclusion of military hardware expenditures that appear to have little or no (or perhaps even negative) effects on improving productivity or creating new marketable products—the two principal sources of growth, not counting education.* Depreciation is estimated by the OMB for all physical capital financed by federal expenditure, which reduces the value of gross investment by about two-thirds, but the *Analyses* makes clear that the appropriate rates of depreciation are uncertain. On the other side of the ledger, the OMB's estimates may be too small. No allowance is made for "consumption" activities that may have a positive effect on growth: we have mentioned armed forces education and the growth effects of health care.

In the face of such uncertainty, we can do little better

---

*On the other hand, there are certainly private investment outlays that also have little or perhaps even negative effects on growth. So there may be a rationale for including military capital on the grounds that what is sauce for the goose is sauce for the gander. We will come back to a similar problem in Chapter 9.

Table 6. Composition of Federal Investment Outlays
($ billions)

	1984	1985	1986	1987	1988 estimate	1989 estimate
Physical investment:						
Direct:						
National defense	68.2	78.0	84.7	89.5	87.5	88.5
Nondefense	9.8	11.7	11.3	12.5	14.2	15.2
Subtotal, direct physical investment	78.0	89.7	95.9	102.1	101.7	103.7
Grants to state and local governments	22.7	24.9	26.3	23.8	25.1	24.9
Subtotal, physical investment	100.7	114.6	122.2	125.9	126.8	128.5
Conduct of research and development:						
National defense	25.8	30.4	35.7	37.1	36.5	39.8
Nondefense	15.2	16.9	16.5	16.2	18.1	19.8
Subtotal, conduct of research and development	41.0	47.2	52.1	53.3	54.6	59.6
Conduct of education and training:						
Direct	11.5	11.6	11.2	11.6	12.2	15.4
Grants to state and local government	10.6	11.4	12.6	12.3	13.4	14.1
Subtotal, conduct of education and training	22.1	23.0	23.7	23.9	25.6	29.5
Loans and financial investments	5.2	32.5	20.5	−2.4	−6.4	−1.2
Other (including commodity inventories)[a]	6.0	5.9	10.9	8.2	5.1	5.9
Total, federal investment outlays	175.0	223.2	229.5	208.9	205.7	222.3
Memorandum						
National defense	94.4	109.6	120.9	126.9	124.3	128.6
Nondefense	80.6	113.6	108.6	82.0	81.4	93.7

[a]Includes a small amount of outlays for private physical investment.
Source: Budget of the United States Government, Special Analyses, FY 1989, Office of Management and Budget, 1988, D-3, Table D-1.

than make the roughest of estimates. Accordingly, for fiscal year 1988 we rule out all military physical investment and accept only OMB's subtotal for nondefense investment outlays (excluding state and local), given as $14.2 billion. Similarly, we exclude all military research, taking only the federal nondefense total of $18.1 billion. We take only the federal education and training investment of $12.2 billion. We ignore the loans and commodity investments (although these have analogs in the private sector's inventory growth), and we reserve a line, without a number on it, to remind us of the absence of any allocation for investment in health and other consumption items noted above. This gives us for 1987:

	$ billions
Net investment	$14.2
Research and development	18.1
Education and training	12.2
Other	—
Total	44.5

This is almost certainly a serious underestimate of the contribution made by the federal government to economic growth, far below the value computed by the OMB. Our calculation is not to be seen as a criticism of the official classification, but rather as a demonstration that even under the most sober and skeptical scrutiny the federal budget includes substantial growth-promoting outlays. In allocating a mere $40 billion capital adjustment to the deficit in Table 5, we have leaned over backward in the interest of conservative accounting. At least this amount deserves to be treated as the public counterpart of private investment for 1987, to be included in the estimates of national capital formation in all calculations. One could easily make a case for a much larger sum.

8

How Big Should a Deficit Be?

THE DEFICIT may be smaller than it appears, but that does not answer the problem that worries many Americans—namely, whatever its true size, the deficit is too big. How does one address such a problem?

Perhaps we can see that that in turn depends on what we use the deficit for. We already know that a deficit—like its identical twin, an increase in debt—can serve two distinct functions. One is to stimulate the economy. The other is to serve as a vehicle for financing capital improvements. Deciding how large a deficit is warranted—including, of course, no deficit or a negative deficit (a surplus)—hinges entirely on these two considerations.

Furthermore, we are also already familiar with the essential considerations behind each of these separate functions. When the economy is taut, a deficit is more likely to accelerate inflation than output. When the economy is slack, it is more likely to add to output than to accelerate inflation. All things considered, then, a first rule of thumb is that deficits are a useful tool of national economic policy when the inflation risk is low, a dangerous tool when the risk is high.

There is, however, a tacit policy decision behind this seemingly innocuous rule. It is that government output should take second place to private output in the order of things. For in an economy running at or near full employment and full plant capacity, *any* additional spending by households or corporations is just as likely to generate inflationary pressures as is spending by government. When we use inflation as a reason for reducing the deficit, we are in fact making a decision to give the private sector the right of way over the public sector—at least, whenever inflation looms.

In the normal course of events, we want the private economy to have such a basic priority. We give enterprise the right of way because private spending in a free-enterprise economy is accorded a widespread and generally unquestioned legitimacy that is never given to the public sector. In *The Wealth of Nations* Adam Smith laid down the three reasons that give public spending such legitimacy as it has: the provision of national defense, the establishment of a magistrate (we would call it law and order), and the provision of needed goods or services that are not profitable for private enterprise to offer—even though, as Smith says, their provision "may frequently do much more than repay [their expenses] to a great society."[13]

But what about the rule of thumb concerning inflation? Might not even Adam Smith's "minimalist" prescription give rise to inflationary tendencies in a fully employed economy? This is an awkward question that we have got around because, in historical fact, capitalism has not been marked, until recent times, by any persisting inflationary trend. Instead, public and private spending have tended to rise together, the public sphere complementing rather than displacing the private. So far as deficit spending has been concerned, war finance excepted, there is no discernible correlation between government borrowing and inflation. As we can see in Table 7, the deficit as a percent of GNP more than doubled during the 1980s, but the inflation rate *fell* by almost a third.*

Suppose, however, that we did face a conflict between our desire to provide public goods and the barrier of inflation. Wartime economies face exactly such problems. Or take a case close to home: suppose a country's infrastructure of transportation and communication systems was falling apart, and the economy was nonetheless uncomfortably near the overheating threshold. Then what do we do?

We use the political process to resolve such economic conflicts. Our elected representatives vote for the neces-

Table 7. Deficits and Inflation, 1954–88

	Annual inflation (%)	Federal deficit as % of GNP
1954–59	2.94	0.18
1960–69	2.73	0.29
1970–79	7.04	1.74
1980–88	4.97	3.86

Source: Economic Report of the President, 1989.

---

*To be precise, the coefficient of correlation from 1954 to 1988 between annual deficits as a percent of GNP and the annual rate of inflation was only 0.20.

sary public projects—perhaps taking adequate measures at the same time to ward off inflation, perhaps not. The basic question of how large the public sector should be—not only what government should do, but how much of the nation's resources it should be able to call on—is a political, not an economic, determination. It is political because there is no way to make such a determination save by political choice.

The political element enters into the determination in two ways. The first and most obvious is the matter we have just discussed, namely, in deciding how much room to give the public sector. This all-important determination, we should note, does not immediately concern the problem of deficit spending. Suppose that we solved the deficit problem by financing all public functions, whether for capital goods or for consumption, through taxation. There would then be no deficit at all.

But that does not mean there would be no political aspect to the government's budget. This budget would still draw the line determining the extent of the public economic domain. Even if it were financed entirely by taxation, the budget would preempt resources that would otherwise have been available to the private sector.

Now let us introduce the question of financing the government's activities by borrowing as well as by taxing. Does this inject a second *political* aspect into the picture? From an Olympian viewpoint it does not. Taxes, like borrowing, are only a means of transferring funds from households and firms to the government. Taxation will no doubt exert different effects on the economy than borrowing, but the differences, as an economist sees them, are only economic.

That may be the way an economist sees things, but it is not the way most households see them. Taxes are regarded as an intrusion by government, whereas the offering of Treasury bonds is not. Borrowing may give rise to frights, but taxes give rise to anger. Households will therefore vote against representatives who seek to tax them to pay for (let us say) roads more readily than they will vote against those who authorize Treasury borrowing. To ask government to finance its capital projects by taxes is accordingly to relegate those projects to the least favorable position in the overall social contest for funds, regardless of their social importance. The public sector will get the taxes needed to run its ordinary expenses, without which the nation might not be able to function; but every project thereafter, *no matter how necessary for economic growth,* will have to face the opposition of the tax-hating public. That is an outcome that very few economists would face with equanimity. They may complain that households ought to be willing to be taxed for the services they want, but that is to express more piety than practical wisdom.*

Thus there is a political side to the deficit question, in that taxes and borrowing are not viewed as indifferently by the public as they are by some economists. Can we not then settle the matter of how large the deficit should be by agreeing to another rule of thumb—namely, to finance by borrowing all growth-related projects and to finance by

---

*Moreover, as economists know, there are powerful reasons to believe that households *will* vote themselves to be undertaxed, because it is in the nature of most government goods and services (like public schools or defense) that they are available to all citizens, whether these particular citizens paid taxes or not. Hence we would expect a polity to undertax itself in the hope of getting a "free ride" on *others'* taxes.

taxing all ordinary expenses? That is an eminently sensible course, both from an economic and a political viewpoint, and it is one that we strongly endorse.

But there is a rub. *There is no way of "matching" our growth-related expenditures to our increase in debt.* Unlike a company whose prospectus for a new bond issue describes in detail the project for which it is intended, no statement of purpose accompanies the issuance of government bonds. It is therefore impossible to match the deficit with public investment! In 1988 for instance, the deficit, as measured in the conventional manner—that is, with no allowance for state and local surpluses or for the effect of inflation—was $162 billion. What was that deficit used for?

No one can say. One could claim that it financed about half the national defense expenditure of $290 billion. Or one might assert that it paid for the net interest cost of $152 billion. Or one could claim that we used it for other purposes such as subsidies for agriculture or old-age pensions—or, for that matter, for the financing of additions to public capital.

There are two important points to be gained from this state of affairs. The first, to which we have referred before and to which we will return in the Appendix to this chapter, is the desirability of breaking down the government's budget into a normal or consumption budget and a capital or growth-related budget. Then all borrowing *could* be matched against capital expenditures, and we could see—and, more important, understand—what the government's borrowing was used for. There may well be many problems in composing such a capital budget—above all, deciding which items belonged in it, with all the political pressures inseparable from such a determination. But better a congressional scramble than the absurd condition that now obtains, in which one can allocate the deficit to any part of the government's expenditure one wishes.

The second point follows directly from the first. Without exception, those who rail against the deficit in fact make such an arbitrary allocation. They blame the deficit for our excessive public consumption—which is to say that they allocate the proceeds of our Treasury's borrowing to such purposes as paying for entitlements like health or social security. If they chose instead to allocate the deficit against investment objectives, the "overspending" on consumption (or the "dissaving," as it is called) would be cut by at least half. The deficit would thereby be vastly reduced, and perhaps eliminated entirely, depending on how one calculated the size of the deficit and public investment spending. More important, fright would be banished from the scene, and the problem of government finance, including the proper size of the deficit, could be discussed in the sober and serious terms to which it is entitled.

APPENDIX

A Capital Budget

What would it take to establish a capital budget? There are many ways of doing so. Here is a framework that lays out one of them:

1. Congress would legislate a capital budget for the national economy, separate from the current budget. Together, the current and the capital budgets would

constitute the total federal budget. The capital budget should probably cover two or four years of projected expenditures, whereas the current budget would cover annual or biannual expenditures.

2. The capital budget would include only appropriations for growth-promoting or growth-related projects. The general criteria for such projects should be established by the legislation establishing the capital budget itself, and a committee, similar to the Congressional Budget Office, would review all such appropriations, calling attention to items that seemed inappropriate.

3. The capital budget would establish the general borrowing authority of the Treasury, beyond which special congressional authorization would be required.

4. The operation of the capital budget would be primarily aimed at strengthening the infrastructural base on which private economic growth and public domestic tranquillity were built. It would certainly include additions to federally-owned plant and equipment, most federally-financed education projects, all federally-sponsored research, and perhaps some expenditures whose purpose was to maintain the health and effectiveness of the work force.

5. Capital projects would be depreciated according to established accounting procedures, and the resulting depreciation charge would become part of the regular current budget.

6. The total volume of capital spending would ordinarily be constrained by the capital budget. Borrowing beyond these limits would hinge on judgments concerning the overall condition of the economy and its need for stim-

ulus. This crucial decision would be proposed by the Council of Economic Advisors and would require congressional approval.

Here it is important not to overstate our case. A capital budget cannot solve, and does not even address, most of the problems that beset America. Capital budgeting does not tell us how to integrate the American economy more successfully into the world economy, or how to improve American productivity to prevent parts of American society from becoming detached from the economic life of the nation.

Nevertheless, whatever course the American economy will take over the future, it is certain to require an intelligent use of federal borrowing and spending, as well as taxing and spending. By making the debt and the deficit comprehensible, capital budgeting allows us to think constructively about problems that otherwise simply benumb our minds. We want to make economics the handmaiden of the electorate, not its inscrutable master.

9

Crowding Out

IF DEFICITS can be benign—even helpful—why is there such a furor about them? There are basically two reasons. The first is that many economists worry that government borrowing will "crowd out" or displace private borrowing. That is a matter for this chapter. The second reason is that many believe that our budget deficit is a symptom of a far more profound problem that might be called a deficit in our ability to generate enough savings. That ties our government deficit to the deficit in our trade relationship with the rest of the world. We will look into the "twin deficits" in the next chapter.

Crowding out is our first concern. It is a very important argument to understand because it is both right, in the terms in which it is couched, and yet, in the final analysis, untenable.

Crowding out is right because it is based on the most widely agreed-upon premise of modern economic analysis: when the demand for any commodity rises, and its supply does not, the price will rise. The crowding-out argument is that deficit spending adds a government demand for savings to an existing private demand—that is, Treasury bonds will seek buyers on top of the bonds issued by private borrowers. The flow of savings is, however, unchanged as a result of the Treasury's entrance into the market. As a result, the price of savings—the rate of interest—must go up. Moreover, if or when the interest rate does go up, the Treasury will not be the borrower that is forced to withdraw from the market. The government is always able to pay any interest rate because of its powers of taxation and money creation. The party that is crowded out is always the private borrower—corporation and/or household.

As with many economic propositions, an argument put in such a precisely spelled-out fashion is invulnerable. If savings are unchanged and government borrowing adds to private borrowing, the interest rate *must* go up when public borrowing is added to private—just as the price of steel must rise if there is an increased demand for steel and an unchanged supply of it.*

Yet there is a curious problem with this inescapable conclusion. In Table 8 we once again examine the performance of the seven major countries we looked at in Table 4. They are ranked, as before, in the order of the rate of growth of their national debts. Canada, at the top of the list, ran the biggest cumulative deficits measured against its GNP; Great Britain, at the bottom, ran the smallest.

All these nations showed increases in their real (inflation-adjusted) interest rates increases from 1980 to 1986,

*The economist will recognize the absence of a few more "ifs"—namely, if the supply of money and people's expectations about the future are also unchanged.

Table 8. Seven Industrial Countries Ranked by Increases in Public Debt and in Real Interest Rates on Government Bonds, 1980–86

Rank in order of debt increase	*Rank in order of increase in interest rates*
1. Canada	1. United Kingdom
2. France	2. Italy
3. Italy	3. France
4. West Germany	4. United States
5. Japan	5. West Germany
6. United States	6. Japan
7. United Kingdom	7. Canada

Source: Peter L. Bernstein, "All the Things Deficits Really Don't Do," *Wall Street Journal,* November 10, 1988.

because their rates of inflation fell faster than the yields on their government bonds. The crowding-out argument would lead us to expect that the countries with the "worst" public debt performance—that is, countries that piled on debt fastest—ought to show the *largest* rise in interest rates, and the countries with the "best" public debt performance the *smallest* rise.

What we see, however, is disconcerting for the proponents of "crowding out." The left-hand column of the table shows how the seven countries ranked in terms of the increase in the public debt-to-income ratios in 1980–86, just as we showed them back in Table 3; the right-hand column shows how they ranked in terms of the relative rise in real interest rates on government bonds. The ordering is very different from what the theory of crowding out would lead us to expect.

The United Kingdom, with the "best" fiscal performance in 1980–86, showed the steepest rise in real rates.

Canada, which has the "worst" debt performance had the best success in holding down real interest rates. The other countries show no significant correlation between interest rate changes and growth in public debt.

In the next chapter we will look into the logic of the argument that connects crowding out with our foreign trade balance and our domestic savings rate. But the simple facts make us very wary of assuming that deficit spending has any clear-cut relation to interest rates. There have been literally dozens of studies of the deficit/interest linkage: some have discovered a relationship; others have not. The most considered judgments seem to conclude, often reluctantly, that crowding out is hard to find. Rudolph Penner, senior fellow at the Urban Institute in Washington and former chief economist of the Congressional Budget Office, has put it this way:

One would expect a positive relationship between the deficit and real interest rates. This relationship has been devilishly difficult to document statistically. Although a majority of studies show a positive relationship, often it is not statistically significant, and some studies show a statistically significant negative relationship. More disturbing, small changes in the specification of the models used can change the relationship from positive to negative and vice versa.[14]

How can we account for the absence of any unambiguous crowding-out effect? Why does not government borrowing increase interest rates, as we would expect in any market where demand increases? Two powerful explanations are available. The first is that the supply of savings is not fixed, as the argument presupposes. The flow of savings varies as national income varies—rising as our total income rises and falling as it falls. Moreover, the flow not only varies along with our income, but with that of other rich nations. The market for attractive national bond issues, such as those issued by the Treasury, is worldwide, not confined to American savers alone.

The second explanation rests on the power of the Federal Reserve System as the controller of the nation's money. A main objective of the Federal Reserve is to use its powers to avert, or at least to lessen, the risk of inflation. This means that when the economy needs brakes because inflation is speeding up, the Federal Reserve uses its powers to raise interest rates and thereby discourage borrowing. On the other hand, when economic conditions are sluggish, the Fed often uses its powers to reduce interest rates, giving a push to business.

These powers of the Federal Reserve are far more influential in determining the course of interest rates than any imaginable crowding out. In 1982, for example, when the U.S. deficit first crossed the hundred-billion mark, interest rates on high-grade corporate bonds were 13.79 percent—between 7 and 8 percent in real terms (after subtracting the 6 percent rate of inflation). By the end of 1987, after five years of deficits totaling a trillion dollars, interest rates had *fallen* to 9.38 percent—about 6 percent in real terms—and the volume of private investment was *up* by about 40 percent. Interest rates fell because inflationary expectations began to wane in response to the fall in oil prices and the Fed's tough stance. This very important change in market expectations persuaded Chairman Paul Volcker of the Federal Reserve that the most serious inflationary threat to the economy had finally disappeared, and that a much-needed policy of "easier" money (lower interest rates and more readily available bank credit) was in order.

Hence, crowding out is a logical scenario that can easily be confounded by changes in the flow of savings or by changes in monetary policy. That is not to say that under certain conditions a real crowding out might not occur, such as when the economy has no unemployed resources and an increase in government demand would therefore force the private sector to move back. Nor is it to deny that government borrowing makes interest rates higher than they would be in the absence of such borrowing. But in the world of practical economic affairs, what counts is where interest rates are—not where they might be if conditions were different. And where interest rates have been and are today is not at all where they would be if government borrowing were crowding out the market for private capital.

We take up the crowding-out argument because it has been talked about so much by economists. But crowding out raises another issue of far greater importance, about which economists have been unaccountably silent: the question of whether crowding out is in itself a sufficient argument for making bad economic policy. Our readers can anticipate our counter argument: Should private spending always have priority over public spending?

One does not have to be an economist to recognize that any kind of ranking of the social or economic value of different kinds of spending is extraordinarily difficult, perhaps even impossible. In the private sector, investors line up at the banks in the order of the profitability of their projects, the most profitable at the head of the line, the least profitable at the end. Yet it is not obvious that a project that yields vast profits—let us say a leveraged buy-out—will yield very large or, for that matter, any positive effects on the national economy. Contrarily, it is equally obvious that many projects whose profit outlook is initially small may turn out to yield huge social as well as private gains.

Evaluating the relative contribution of public projects is at least as difficult. Some public investments are monuments of waste and some are cornucopias of plenty. Consider on the one hand the nuclear plants built by the government, and on the other the Institutes of Health or the Agricultural Extension program. Most projects are probably in between, with complex chains of secondary and tertiary influence: military research may be one such. We cannot line up such a variety of projects in order of their worth. And even supposing we could do so, how are we to mix the two lines of would-be borrowers—one private, one public—into one rationally ordered queue at the nation's savings window?

The answer is that we cannot make any such queue, and we do not even try to do so. Instead, we simply put all public projects at the head of the queue, because we know that the Treasury will indeed be able to pay whatever the market demands to secure the needed funds. Thereafter, private borrowers line up in order of profitability. The crowding-out critics are therefore correct in maintaining that government projects will have first crack at the nation's savings.

Their argument becomes untenable when they fail to put forward any other way of rationing the nation's savings. If the critics declared that crowding out was a poor policy *after necessary public investment had been taken care of,* or if they declared that *private investment was always more important for national growth and well-being than any kind of public spending,* our counterargument would collapse, for in both cases the critics would have supplied a rationale, convincing or not, as to the relative importance of public versus private spending.*

Lacking any such rationale, an opposition to crowding out implies that the right place for government is at the end of the line, even if this leaves nothing at all for public purposes. We can then pay for our public capital by taxation alone, making do with a smaller stock of new capital if taxation generates much greater public opposition than borrowing. Or perhaps we can persuade citizens of the need for public capital, so that they will acquiesce in the taxes to build all our needed capital, with no borrowing. That will end the argument about crowding out—*until someone asks whether increased taxation is not also crowding out private spending as effectively as any rise in interest rates!*

Thus the crowding-out argument leads inescapably to the conclusion that public investment has no intrinsic legitimacy. If it is crowding out that we wish to avoid, we have no option but to put all private expenditures before

---

*A few economists, who have the courage of their convictions, are indeed willing to relegate government to the end of the line, vital functions such as defense or law and order excepted. Milton Friedman is among them. Having gratefully availed ourselves of his support earlier, it is with regret that we must part company here.

any public spending. If we object to the present budget process because it puts the public sector at the head of the line, we are forced to support a procedure that moves the government to the rear of the line.

Is there any reasonable solution to this dilemma? Yes and no. No, in that there is no workable alternative to the present system in which our elected representatives vote for a government budget financed by both taxes and borrowing. This system does indeed assert the priority of government spending over that of private spending, in that the government's claim on the national purchasing power is always greater than that of the private economy, whether the government gathers its funds by its power to tax or to borrow.

There is, however, a very important matter to be borne in mind. As we mentioned above, crowding out applies only to a full-employment economy. Government spending, financed by taxes or by borrowing, will shoulder aside private spending only when we are at or near full employment, so that every dollar spent for a public project must shoulder aside a dollar from a private one. When we have unused resources, government does not crowd out private spending, but encourages it.

So, yes, there *is* a reasonable solution to the crowding-out dilemma. It is to accept the priority of government as the first claimant on resources as the only practicable way in which a democratic capitalist society can create a public space within the larger private economy. Modern capitalism allows the government to go first because it would be a disaster to have government go last—just suppose there were no funds for defense, for law and order, for any public goods!—and because there is no automatic, marketlike way of combining both sectors into one. In so doing, we rely on the good sense of Congress not to extend government's reach beyond that which is sanctioned by the electorate. Through our normal democratic processes, Congress then determines how the government sector is to be financed. Normally this is done partly by taxation, partly by borrowing.

Does this not raise the danger that government may encroach on the private economy to the point at which government suffocates or even extinguishes the private system? There is certainly a long-run drift toward an enlargement of the public sector, mainly because entitlement spending has expanded so much in the twentieth century. Few would deny that this enlargement of the public sphere has changed capitalism, but few would maintain that capitalism has been undermined by it. As for the position of the United States in this historical drift, we are far from being a leader. As Benjamin Friedman writes:

The total share of government activity in America in 1987, including the federal level as well as state and local governments, even including the interest on all government debt, was only 35 percent [of gross national product]. Comparable government shares in European countries are 48 percent in Germany, 46 percent in Britain, and 50 percent in France. Only in Japan, where the corresponding share is typically 29 to 30 percent . . . , is the the government any smaller compared to the economy.[15]

Can we sum up the complex question of crowding out? The issue turns out to have little to do with deficit spending but a great deal to do with how we feel about the role of government in a capitalist economy. For at its core, crowding out boils down to the relative size of private and public spending. It is as simple—and as complex—as that. As is so often the case, Herbert Stein has taken the measure of this problem. He writes:

> The case for saying that expenditures in general are too high seems to rest on two propositions. One is that government expenditures constitute an infringement of the freedom of private parties to use their own income and may pave the way for the infringement of other freedoms as well. The other is that government expenditures are inherently excessive and wasteful because they are made or influenced by people who are not spending their own money. Each of these arguments is open to two qualifications. In the first place they are clearly not applicable to all kinds of expenditures, which raises the problem of choosing which to cut and even raises the possibility that the complaint is inconsequential for some expenditures relative to the benefit from the expenditure. Second, the arguments seem to have been as applicable to the federal budget of Calvin Coolidge, 3 percent of GNP, as to the budget of Ronald Reagan, 22 percent of GNP. Indeed, the arguments seem to run against having any government expenditure at all.[16]

This issue will always loom large in capitalism, which alone in history boasts a sphere of private as well as a sphere of public economic undertakings. The determination of the dividing line between the two spheres will be influenced by whether we use taxes or borrowing to pay for our public activities, for borrowing avoids the political resistance that is likely to accompany taxation. Therefore, deficit spending may be the most expedient manner in which a nation can undertake large-scale or long-lasting programs whose payoff in growth may not be immediately evident. That, we can see, is a matter for reasonable people to agree or disagree about. It is not a matter in which fear or fright need enter.

10

Living Beyond
Our Means

Our main interest up to this point has been to understand the meaning—and to take an accurate measure—of the federal deficit. Along the way, we have also explored a crucial concern that lies hidden in the deficit: the competition between government spending and private investment.

Now our screen widens. The deficit remains our central focus, but the consequences of the deficit grow larger and more important—indeed, more important than anything we have discussed so far. For the most serious and thoughtful critics of the deficit problem assert that our fiscal policies are causing us to live beyond our means.

The first symptom of this problem is our savings shortfall. By spending more of the national income than it collects in taxes, the government appears to divert savings away from the private investment that is essential if economic growth is to continue. If that charge could be substantiated, it would override—or at the very least severely qualify—everything we have presented so far to lower anxieties about the federal deficit.

The second symptom is found in the persistent failure of

the United States to balance its international accounts. The deficit in our national savings, which shows up as the unprecedented excess of federal expenditures over revenues, is said to lead to the deficit in our dealings in foreign trade, which shows up as the unprecedented excess of imports over exports.*

The similarities in movements between these two deficits have earned them the name of the "twin deficits." Our first task is to understand the nature of this linkage, to see how there can be a connection between what the federal government does by way of taxing and spending and what the mass of business and consumers do as they collectively buy from or sell to foreigners.

Let us follow the answer of those who worry about the unholy twins. Their response usually begins with a question: Can a household live better than the value of its own contribution to production—that is, can it spend more than its own earnings? Of course it can. A household that wants to spend more than its income can find additional money to spend by borrowing, by drawing down its bank deposits, or by selling securities and other assets. That is what we usually mean by "living beyond our means."

As with individual households, so with the totality of households, the nation itself. Suppose that most Americans choose to live beyond their means, outborrowing those who choose to save. Then the nation as a whole

---

*We content ourselves with one ringing statement of the danger of the twin deficits. Here is Paul Samuelson, dean of the American economics profession and winner of the Nobel Prize: "The proximate cause of the chronic balance-of-payments deficits . . . is the new devil in American life—the basic structural federal deficit. . . . The evil of a basic structural deficit is that it is the devil's recipe for a low-saving economy." (*Harvard Business Review,* November/December 1988)

would find that it had gone into debt or sold off its assets. But if most of us are borrowing or selling our stocks and bonds, *from whom* can we borrow and *to whom* can we sell? There can be only one answer: the lenders and the buyers must be foreigners. In short, a nation that lives beyond its means is both buying more than it produces— that is, importing more than it exports—and borrowing the money from abroad to do so.

In addition, the phrase "living beyond our means" has a second connotation when applied to the nation as a whole. The words are used to describe a country that fails to generate enough savings to support its own capital investment. This is the point at which the deficits become twins, for the claim is that the budget deficit, by absorbing the savings needed to support investment, forces the nation to make up the buying-and-producing deficit by importing and borrowing from abroad.

This is exactly what Table 9 seems to indicate. The arithmetic of the table is undeniable.* The shortfall is real. Business and households together saved $723 billion ($141 plus $584 billion). That is, they spent $723 billion less on current consumption and operating expenses than their current incomes and revenues. But this saving was reduced by the $82 billion of *dissaving* by the public sector— the excess of total expenditures over tax revenues by all arms of government, state and local as well as federal.

At the bottom of the table, we see that the United States

---

*Note that the figures in this table refer to calendar 1988, not to fiscal 1988. We make this change for two reasons: first to make the calculations as up to date as possible, and second to accustom the reader to differences that arise from the use of fiscal and calendar figures—a frequent source of confusion in using government statistics. The variances between fiscal and calendar for 1988 are small. The message is the same.

Table 9. Saving and Investment in the U.S. Economy, 1988[a]

	($ billions)
Consumer saving	141
Business saving	582
Government saving	−82
Total national saving	*641*
Business investment	765
Net savings deficit	*−124*
Memo: Net foreign deficit (net imports)	−131

[a]First nine months at annual rate.
Source: Economic Report of the President, 1989, Table B-28.

imported $134 billion more than it exported. In other words, we did live beyond our means to that extent in 1988.

But what is the linkage between this trade deficit and the deficit incurred by the federal government? The table purports to provide us with the answer. The dissaving by the government sector appears to be a sponge that mops up $82 billion that would otherwise have been available for the private sector. Actually, the dissaving of the *federal* government alone was $137 billion. Had the federal government not overspent its income, our total savings would have amounted to $778 billion, or more than enough to cover the investment needs of the business sector.

Is this calculation ironclad proof that there is a real twin deficit problem?

Yes and no. Yes, because there may well be a problem of insufficient saving in the United States and there is surely too large an import surplus. No, because that is not the same thing as pinning all the blame on the federal government's fiscal policy. For instance, if the federal government had spent less and raised taxes in order to eliminate its dissaving, there would also have been less consumer and business saving, because their incomes would probably have been smaller. Balancing the budget would have rectified the shortage of saving *only on the unlikely supposition that consumers and business firms made absolutely no changes in their decisions to spend, save, and invest in spite of lower government revenues and higher taxes.*

Moreover, the figure of $82 billion for net government dissaving is itself open to serious question. We probably know what is wrong with it. It does not recognize any public investment.

Yet, as we have seen, a cautious estimate of public investment for 1988 comes to about $100 billion—$55 billion by states and municipalities and at least $40 billion by the federal government. The table, however, shows that all this money spent on roads, bridges, buildings, research, and education was written off as though the value of these projects was totally used up during the course of 1988. By this method of accounting, the business sector would also show a "deficit," for business spent $183 billion more than its own savings in 1988. By the same token, total government tax revenues for the year ($1,556 billion) less all government noninvestment spending ($1,538 billion) now shows government saving of $18 billion.

Therefore, we can reconstruct our table to create Table 10. The change is startling. We are still not living within our means, but now the reason is clear. The need for all investment, public and private, is $124 billion greater than the amount of saving generated by all three sectors. But we can no longer assert that the budget deficit is to blame! As we know from our examination of crowding out, public

**Table 10. Saving and Investment in the
U.S. Economy, 1988, Revised**

($ billions)

Consumer saving	141
Business saving	582
Government saving	18
Total national saving	*741*
Business investment	765
Government investment	100
Total investment	*865*
Net savings deficit	−124
Memo: Net foreign deficit	−131

investment cannot take a back seat to private investment. Indeed, very possibly economic growth would suffer more if we failed to provide for our public capital needs than if we cut back on our private needs.

Furthermore, the conventional approach to the savings shortfall is blind at another critically important point: it treats the import surplus as a total drain on growth. All of the borrowings of Americans from foreigners, in other words, are treated as a net deduction from our wealth, leaving us poorer for our efforts. Yet our imports in 1988 included nearly $120 billion of machinery, aircraft, and trucks. These capital goods accounted for 29 percent of our total merchandise imports, up from only 20 percent in 1980.

If our revised table included these investment items, they would further alter its meaning. We would then see that we are borrowing from foreigners, or selling them assets, to acquire productive capital, not just Italian shoes or Saudi oil. That is hardly an exchange that makes us poorer. As long as our total investment in capital goods, purchased abroad as well as domestically produced, exceeds the amount that we are borrowing from foreigners, we are adding to our wealth on balance, not heading toward poverty and bankruptcy.*

Nevertheless, some people do worry about foreigners becoming disillusioned with the United States and provoking a flight from the dollar; others worry about foreigners owning too much of the United States. We have already touched on this matter in Chapter III. Suffice it to say that foreigners will continue to want to hold dollar assets as long as Americans want to hold dollar assets—as long, that is, as we maintain an economic environment congenial to enterprise. That seems like a sound bet.

And as for the fear that foreigners are soon going to "own us," this is only a fright for an economy whose total assets are worth about $15 trillion, not even counting land and human resources. Foreigners own less than 2 percent of U.S. commercial real estate, less than 1 percent of our farmland, and only 4 percent of our corporate stock.[17]

But the twin deficits are not only mismeasured. Their linkage is misconceived. Cutting the budget deficit will not, in simple mechanical fashion, alter our propensity to import or the willingness of foreigners to buy the goods we produce. The trade deficit is driven by its own set of forces, such as economic trends outside the United States and differentials in costs and marketing skills—not to mention a highly developed American taste for foreign goods.

For example, the need to repay their dollar-denomi-

---

*The official statistics state that about $500 billion of our $765 billion of business investment in 1988 was to replace worn-out equipment. Nevertheless, this estimate of *net* investment exceeds the inflow of foreign capital. This calculation also assumes that the new capital goods were no more productive than the capital goods they replaced. And once again, it also totally excludes public or household sector investment.

nated debts has decimated Latin American markets for American exports. The fall in the price of oil since the early 1980s has forced a steep cut in OPEC purchases of U.S. merchandise. Can cutting the federal deficit restore the dollar purchasing power of these erstwhile customers?

Or can cutting the federal deficit narrow the wage gap between the U.S. manufacturing wage of $13 an hour and the $2.50 an hour earned by manufacturing workers in Hong Kong, Taiwan, Singapore, and Korea? Can it bring back to the United States the manufacturing facilities that have fled abroad to low-wage countries? Are our budget deficits responsible for the fact that economic growth in western Europe and Japan was so sluggish from 1982 to 1986?

In other words, the twin-deficit theory may have *reversed* the actual process of cause and effect. Instead of the federal budget deficit causing the trade deficit, perhaps the trade deficit caused the budget deficit. As suggested above, had we bought more of our own output and sold more abroad during the 1980s, American employment, incomes, and profits would have been higher during the 1980s than in fact they were—the resources for this extra production were readily available in the United States until at least the middle of 1987, and probably longer. Then government revenues would also have been higher and government dissaving correspondingly smaller.[18]

As a result of these reversible causalities, a balanced federal budget may not provide the cure for the trade deficit that so many people expect of it. It certainly will not provide such a cure if a reduction in domestic demand from higher taxes or lower government spending does not result in lower imports. What if fiscal prudence causes households to give up a winter vacation in Florida while they continue to enjoy their summer vacations in France, or to buy a Hyundai instead of a Honda?

Thus there can be no automatic assurance that efforts to boost the national rate of saving will accomplish their goal. The 1989 annual report of the Council of Economic Advisors aptly sums up the matter:

A deficit absorbs saving but actually affects the total saving in the economy in a complex manner. Because the federal deficit, interest rates, output, and prices are part of an interdependent system, it is incorrect to assume that a dollar reduction in the budget deficit would add an equal amount to gross saving. . . . The balance of trade deficits of recent years and consequent flow of foreign saving into the United States constitute a combined result of forces influencing both the government budget deficit and private incentives to save and invest.[19]

In short, changes in private sector variables, just as changes in taxes and government spending, must be accompanied by the appropriate changes in the other variables if any new policy is to yield the results we seek.*

This is not quite all, however. The problem deserves one last look. The twin deficit case rests on a simple proposition: the budget deficit absorbs the savings that would oth-

---

*An elegant analysis of these complexities is to be found in Friedman's *Day of Reckoning,* pp. 270–300. Although he is keenly aware of the reverse causalities referred to above, Friedman is vehemently opposed to deficit spending at this time, adamant in his belief that it represents only dissaving and that it is sapping our ability to save and invest. It seems to us that the only way in which Professor Friedman can maintain this position is by the assumption that the purposes for which the government borrows are of less economic value than those for which the business sector borrows. This is an odd conclusion in view of his sympathetic view of the need for government spending in general (p. 286) and for infrastructure in particular (pp. 204–6).

erwise be available to the private sector. The deficit is the reason that we are living beyond our means and importing so much more than we export.

We have seen many weaknesses in this claim. There is one more: the theory accords uneasily with the facts. A comparison across seven major countries shows no systematic pattern linking their budget deficits to changes in their international accounts.

Table 11 ranks these seven countries twice. The ranking in the left-hand column lists them in order of the relative size of the cumulative government deficits they ran from 1980 to 1986; the ranking in the right-hand column lists them with the countries whose international accounts deteriorated the most on top and the countries whose international accounts improved the most on the bottom. If the theory held true, the order in which the seven countries appear would be the same in both columns. But the

Table 11. Ranking of Seven Industrial Countries Based on Cumulative Changes in Government Debt and in International Accounts, 1980–86

Ranking based on increase in government debt/GNP[a]	Ranking based on deterioration in international accounts/GNP
1. Canada	1. United States
2. France	2. Italy
3. Italy	3. France
4. West Germany	4. Canada
5. Japan	5. West Germany
6. United States	6. United Kingdom
7. United Kingdom	7. Japan

[a]Ratio includes local as well as central government units.
Source: Table 3 and International Monetary Fund.

facts do not fit the theory very well. Canada and the United States are all out of order; Japan is two places out of order; and not one country is ranked the same in both columns!

How can logic be right and be contradicted by the facts? The economist calls on an essential condition for all theory—*ceteris paribus* or "all other things equal." Logical connections provide linkages when everything else is static. Unfortunately for theory, that is not the real world.

What remains, then, of the savings question after we have set aside the twin deficits? The answer is that the low savings rate remains—low compared to our own past performance, and low compared to other countries. Like other countries, however, our savings rate is not specifically a function of government finance.* Rather, a nation's disposition *and its ability* to save are a reflection of the overall character of the economy and the society.

Many studies have shown a strong association between high national savings rates and high rates of growth in output and productivity. This does not prove that the high savings rates were the cause of outstanding economic performance. On the contrary, the entire history of economic development around the world demonstrates that a nation is able to consume less than it produces only when production is outpacing the growth in basic human needs. It is no coincidence that the low national savings rates in the United States in the 1980s were accompanied by the slow growth in real household incomes that we mentioned

---

*An array similar to that in Table 11, but based on the change in government debt and the change in savings ratios, also shows no systematic pattern of any kind.

above, or by a ratio of corporate profits to GNP only half what it was in the 1960s and 1970s.

In real terms, consumption grew at an annual rate of 3.0 percent from the end of 1979 to the end of 1988. This was even less than during the difficult 1970s and far below the growth rate of consumption in the ebullient 1950s and 1960s. Hence, the low rate of household savings is a result of the sluggish growth in real purchasing power. Had total incomes after taxes and adjusted for inflation grown during the 1980s at the same rate as during the 1970s (which was well below the 1960s), personal saving in 1988 would have been more than double the amount shown in Table 11.

Much the same may be true of business saving. Without the intensely competitive business conditions imposed by the flood of imports, corporate profitability would surely have been much higher during the 1980s than it was—and so would investment and the growth of productivity.

The issue, then, is whether we view economic growth as a problem or as the solution. Putting the matter in these terms suggests the proper answer to the question of whether we can raise our national savings rate by cutting the budget deficit. The answer is no if that will result in a further squeeze on household and business income. The answer is yes if at the same time we are committed to measures to improve the productivity and international competitiveness of the American economy. And the achievement of these goals is critically dependent on a high level of public as well as private investment.

What, then, to do about it? We propose a two-step approach.

First, by all means balance the government's *operating* budget—total government spending less total government investment—if and when the operating budget is in deficit.* This can be done by cutting noninvestment spending, with defense the most likely candidate, and by raising taxes, with gasoline as the most promising immediate target.

Second, increase public investment by borrowing. A deficit used for public capital formation is the best way to raise household and business income, and, therefore, household and business saving. Deficits used for investment do not "absorb" savings, they generate savings.

---

*In calendar 1988, let us recall, the federal government's operating budget *was* in balance.

II

False Alarms and
Real Possibilities

IT IS TIME to recapitulate the argument. Let us do so in terms of some of the specific false alarms to which it has been addressed, and some of the central points we have tried to establish.

1. *Our present chronic deficit is not the result of profligacy.* It is the unexpected consequence of our vigorous and successful—perhaps too vigorous, but blessedly successful—efforts to fight inflation through an extremely tight money policy. The consequence has been a deadly combination of forces—a ballooning of entitlements inherited from the inflation behind us, a slowing down of tax receipts from the recession into which we entered, and a startling increase in interest costs that tight money forced upon us. We are not likely to encounter such a deadly combination again.

2. *The national debt is not a net national liability.* It is the sum of the outstanding obligations issued by the Treasury, "backed" by the productive power and the real human and physical assets, of the nation.

3. *The national debt is not large, measured by historical or international comparisons.* All modern economies have national debts among whose useful purposes is to provide to private investors a vehicle that carries the full faith and credit of the issuing government. Our present debt is roughly 43 percent of our gross national product. This ratio is about the same proportion as in 1940, and puts us well within the debt-to-GNP ratios of our industrial competitors.

4. *The burden of the debt will not impoverish our grandchildren.* The great bulk of the interest we pay on the national debt is a transfer from American taxpayers to American interest receivers. If we ever repaid the debt, the generation that would have to pay it off would be the same generation that would receive the proceeds. Furthermore, instead of paying off the debt, it makes more sense to refinance maturing debt with new obligations to replace those that have matured.

5. *A deficit is not necessarily a drain on our well-being.* On the contrary, a deficit can have two very positive functions. It can serve as a stimulus when the national economy needs one. And it can provide a convenient and sensible means of financing capital undertakings.

6. *The deficit is not bigger than we think: it is smaller.* There are many criteria by which we can calculate the increase in the national debt—that is, the deficit. The most commonly used measure does not adjust for the effects of inflation, and it treats all government expenditure as consumption, rather than recognizing that at least 5 percent and perhaps as much as 20 percent of it is investment.

7. *A rational budget would place government expenditures on capital goods in a separate capital account, rather*

than charging them against income. We would then seek to hold our normal operating budget within our tax revenues, as a household or a corporation seeks to hold its normal expenditures within its income; and ordinarily we would issue bonds only to finance capital improvements, including education and perhaps some rehabilitative expenditures. The deficit, as we know it, would disappear from our concerns. In its place would come a proper concern: for what purposes and to what extent do we wish to borrow in order to expand or strengthen our public infrastructure?

8. *The relation of deficit spending to private investment, private saving, and our foreign trade deficit is far from clear.* Expenditures financed by government borrowing may or may not force up interest rates, and this may or may not be contrary to the national interest, depending on which projects are pushed aside. A national deficit may or may not siphon off national savings, depending on the state of our economy. Like the crowding-out argument, much depends on recognizing and evaluating the investment component within the deficit. The linkage between domestic deficits and foreign deficits is similarly uncertain in that the foreign deficit may be the cause, not the consequence, of our government deficit. Moreover, the foreign deficit, like the domestic one, contains an important investment component. Neither can be cavalierly treated as dissaving.

Thus, to repeat what we said at the outset, by no stretch of the imagination can "reducing the deficit" be considered as America's number-one problem, as it *is* considered by 44 percent of the population and probably by a larger percent of economists. If it were America's number-one problem, we would be very well off indeed.

What are America's most pressing economic problems? To our mind the gravest is to integrate the American economy successfully into the world economy. Our import surplus makes clear that if we do not resolve this problem ourselves, the forces of the market will resolve it for us by narrowing and compressing America's place as a world manufacturer and industrial pioneer. Another name for this vitally important challenge is to restore American competitiveness.

Perhaps the second gravest issue is to find some method of controlling the inflationary threat that affects the American economy like a subacute infection—not quite serious but always there, ready to flare up into a really debilitating condition. The problem with this affliction is not so much the damage it does, but that it turns vigorous private growth or vigorous public policy into problems rather than solutions. Every time "good statistics" come out of Washington the market drops, sensing another Federal Reserve massacre around the corner.

High on any list is the critical need to arrest the decay of urban life and to perform the microsurgery needed to restore economic circulation to the bottom tenth of the population. The restoration of environmental balance obviously belongs on the list of pressing economic problems. So do reform of our stock market casino and restraint in the game of corporate civil war. And we have left out a dozen other candidates, most egregiously the revitalization of American education, without which our most important source of productivity—our store of intelligence—is allowed to go to waste, a true national disaster.

What is immediately apparent is that some, but not all, of these major challenges require substantial government finance. Our place in the international system, our domestic price stability, our corporate conduct, will hinge primarily on our capacity for institutional adaptation rather than on money. That is not necessarily a reason for rejoicing—money may be much easier to come by than institutional innovation and flexibility.

Other problems are more expensive. Environmental control already demands massive deployment of labor and capital, and from what we know of the extent of our nuclear containment problem alone, it will make increasing demands in the future. The repair of city life and the microsurgery of job creation will need large amounts of money, although money without good institutional vehicles is likely to produce disappointing results. Education is expensive, much more expensive than we have been willing to admit. And the American economy may again need an ongoing stimulus from government spending, as it has in the past, using the borrowing and spending powers of the government to bring us to a satisfactory level of employment and income.

Thus many real challenges of our time may call for considerable government spending, and if they do there seems no possibility, given the public's aversion to being taxed, that this spending can be mounted without borrowing. Does this not return us to square one? Frights and false alarms aside, can we live indefinitely with a policy of government borrowing and spending?

This is a question we have asked before, but it deserves a second examination. Suppose that the net debt of the nation—for convenience's sake, let us say measured in the conventional way—rises roughly parallel to our increase in output. If real output grows at a rate of 2.5 percent a year (approximately our historical rate) it will double roughly every 30 years. By 2020, GNP will be $10 trillion; by 2050, $20 trillion. It follows from our assumption that our debt will reach $4 trillion by the year 2020, and $8 trillion 30 years further down the road. And these numbers pay no heed to inflation. Suppose that our cost of living also rises at 2.5 percent a year, a very modest figure. Then everything must be doubled again. By 2020 we will have a debt of $8 trillion, by 2050, one of $16 trillion.

Are these numbers to tremble at? They are not. We have assumed that our debt will rise parallel to our gross national product. If we recall the impetus to productivity associated with public capital spending, there seems no reason to question this assumption. As we have previously seen, this means that a tax structure resembling that of today ought easily to generate the revenues needed to pay the interest on that debt—an interest bill growing in size, but not in proportion to our wealth and income.

But suppose that debt rises *faster* than GNP; or that the rate of interest increases, so that even a steadily growing debt costs ever more to service; or that foreigners increase their share of the debt by a very large amount. There is no question that any of these possibilities would make the management of our debt much more difficult. Interest could then swell to the point at which it becomes a real political item in our tax bills, or our payments to foreigners could begin to pose the same difficulties for us that they do to Mexico or Brazil today.

Such scenarios could have many outcomes, all of them unpleasant to one degree or another. Before we consider them, let us conjure up another set of unpleasant possibilities. Suppose that TV proves to be too much for the counter pull of education, so that our national board scores for math and physics remain an international disgrace. Suppose that American society comes apart at the seams—Wall Street indistinguishable from Atlantic City, the cities laced with barricades. Suppose that American management never learns how to treat its workforce as an asset, not a liability. These suppositions also point to national prospects of a disheartening or disruptive kind—but none of them presupposes a federal deficit.

The point is that unintelligent or unimaginative policies, or inertia and insensitivity, can have as grave effects in the private sector as in the public sector. It is of course possible to imagine that the national government will conduct its fiscal affairs in a reckless or heedless fashion, just as it is possible to imagine that public morality and business ingenuity will prove inadequate to the tasks they must undertake. We prefer to place expectations in the middle range of possibilities, expecting neither miracles nor disasters from government or from business. Managing a debt will of necessity impose problems, but not insuperable problems—just as is apt to be the case with managing the private sector. Utilizing the growth-promoting capabilities of the government will provide real possibilities, but not cure-alls—just as realizing the capacity for private growth will provide the basis for national well-being, but will not in itself provide that well-being.

Thus the great problems remain far deeper, more obdurate, less easily described than any arrangement of government finance. But government finance, including borrowing and spending, is likely to be part of the redress we can apply to these problems.

What does that finally imply by way of a conclusion for our primer? Our answer will be very brief and not at all surprising.

In normal times we favor a "deficit", by which we mean growth-promoting expenditures on a capital budget, of 2 to 3 percent of GNP—perhaps $100 billion to $150 billion at today's values.

And that is all. The lesson is over. If we have been successful, this general program, which might have come as a shock before our argument was heard, will now appear as a common-sensical, even modest proposal, measured against the nation's needs. There will be no ringing of alarm bells, but we hope, a sense that our national finances are, after all, within our grasp.

Notes

1. Milton Friedman, "Why the Twin Deficits Are a Blessing," *Wall Street Journal,* December 14, 1988; Walter B. Wriston, remarks at the Business Council, October 8, 1988; and Herbert Stein, "Now, Please, Can We Begin to Discuss the Budget?" *The Economist,* American Enterprise Institute, December 1988.
2. John H. Makin, "The Reagan Years: A Fiscal Perspective," *The Economist,* American Enterprise Institute, April 1988.
3. Friedman, "Why the Twin Deficits Are a Blessing."
4. Goldman, Sachs, *The Pocket Chartroom,* December 1988, p. C.11; *Statistical Abstract of the United States,* 1988, Tables 722, 793, 795, 809, 816, 846, 858, 865.
5. *Statistical Abstract,* Table 722.
6. Friedman, "Why the Twin Deficits Are a Blessing."
7. *Statistical Abstract,* Tables 725, 726.
8. Benjamin Friedman, *Day of Reckoning,* Random House, New York, 1988, p. 88.
9. David Alan Aschauer, "Rx for Productivity: Build Infrastructure," *Chicago Fed Letter,* September 1988.
10. *Economic Report of the President,* Table B-79. Also Robert Eisner, *How Real Is the Federal Deficit?* Free Press, New York, 1986, Table 5.2, p. 52.
11. Stephin Entin, "Real Deficits and the NEC's Real Duty," *Wall Street Journal,* December 1, 1988.
12. Eisner, *How Real Is the Federal Deficit?* pp. 17, 20; Friedman, *Day of Reckoning,* p. 88.
13. Adam Smith, *The Wealth of Nations,* Modern Library, New York, 1936, p. 651.
14. *Business Economics,* October 1988, p. 8. See also *Economic Report of the*

Notes

President, 1985, p. 38; Frederick Mishkin, *Understanding Real Interest Rates,* National Bureau of Economic Research Working Paper #2691, August 1988.
15. Friedman, *Day of Reckoning,* p. 286.
16. Herbert Stein, "Now, Please, Can We Begin to Discuss the Budget?"
17. See John H. Makin, "Japan's Investment in America: Is It a Threat?" *Challenge,* November/December 1988; Peter A. Lewis, "Let the Yen, Pounds and Marks Pour In," *New York Times,* January 21, 1989.
18. See Robert A. Blecker and Alan G. Isaac, "Technological Change and International Competitiveness," American Economic Association meetings, December 1988.
19. *Economic Report of the President,* 1989, p. 98.

Index

Index

Index

ROBERT HEILBRONER is the author of many books and articles, ranging from his famous *The Worldly Philosophers* to an exploration of *The Nature and Logic of Capitalism* (1985), and from much-discussed pieces in *The New Yorker* to scholarly essays in academic journals. Long associated with the New School for Social Research, where he is Norman Thomas Professor of Economics, he has lectured at over one hundred universities and has received many honors, including election as vice president of the American Economic Association in 1984. He is married and lives in New York City and Bridgehampton, New York.

PETER BERNSTEIN is an economic consultant to institutional investors and corporations, and publisher of "Economics and Portfolio Strategy," a semi-monthly analysis of the capital markets.

A graduate of Harvard, he is a former member of the research staff of the Federal Reserve Bank of New York as well as of the Williams College faculty. He was a practicing investment counsel from 1951 to 1973 and has served as a trustee and member of the Finance Committee of the College Retirement Equities Fund (CREF). Mr. Bernstein is also editor of the *Journal of Portfolio Management* and the author of four books on economics and finance and many articles in professional and popular journals. In 1983, Mr. Bernstein received the Silbert Annual Economics Forecasting Award for accuracy, timeliness, and professionalism in economic forecasting.

He is married and has homes in New York City and Brattleboro, Vermont.